ALMOST CHRISTMAS

A WESLEYAN
ADVENT EXPERIENCE

MAGREY R. DEVEGA · INGRID MCINTYRE
APRIL CASPERSON · MATT RAWLE

LARGE PRINT

Abingdon Press
Nashville

Almost Christmas
A Wesleyan Advent Experience
Large Print

ISBN 978-1-5018-9059-8

Scripture quotations unless noted otherwise are taken from the Common English Bible, copyright 2011. Used by permission. All rights reserved.

Scripture quotations noted NRSV are from the New Revised Standard Version Bible, copyright © 1989 National Council of the Churches of Christ in the United States of America. Used by permission. All rights reserved worldwide. http://nrsvbibles.org/

Scripture quotation noted (NIV) is taken from the Holy Bible, New International Version®, NIV®. Copyright © 1973, 1978, 1984, 2011 by Biblica, Inc.™ Used by permission of Zondervan. All rights reserved worldwide. www.zondervan.com The "NIV" and "New International Version" are trademarks registered in the United States Patent and Trademark Office by Biblica, Inc. ™

Hymn numbers are from *The United Methodist Hymnal* (Nashville, TN: The United Methodist Publishing House, 1989).

19 20 21 22 23 24 25 26 27 28—10 9 8 7 6 5 4 3 2 1
MANUFACTURED IN THE UNITED STATES OF AMERICA

CONTENTS

Additional resources, including Advent and Nativity hymn suggestions, litanies for lighting the Advent wreath, and prayers that can be used in worship and small group settings are available at **https://www.abingdonpress.com /Almost-Christmas-Downloads.**

INTRODUCTION

In a particular episode of the classic comic strip *Dennis the Menace*, Dennis is standing in the living room on Christmas morning, brightly decorated tree in the corner, with stacks of empty boxes and shreds of wrapping paper all around him. Having opened up his mountains of Christmas gifts, he stands there, arms outstretched and yelling at the top of his lungs for all in the house to hear: "Is that all?"

Of course, we want to tell Dennis that he missed the point. We'd prefer to remember that Christmas is not about receiving presents, checking off your wish lists, and getting everything you want. Despite what holiday retailers would want us to believe, Black Friday does not define Christmas Day.

Yet, if we are honest, we do find ourselves resonating at a certain level with dear Dennis. As we go through a December filled with the frenzy of gift-buying, party planning, house cleaning, home decorating, and one-social-gathering-after-another, we can see ourselves stepping back from the madness of it and saying to ourselves, "Is that all?" Is this all there is to

Christmas? Isn't there something more that should define our observance of this season?

As it turns out, there is. Tell that Dennis the Menace inside you to look under the tree one more time, because there is a gift that you may not have noticed before, and your name is on it. But notice that it's not next to the "To:" line. It's next to the "From:" line.

This gift is not for you. It's intended to come *from* you. It is not a gift for you to open; it is a gift for you to deliver. It is a gift for God, and it is the gift of yourself.

It is the gift of your wholehearted, freely given commitment to God, allowing God to shape your life in the way that God intends. Many of the main characters in the story of the birth of Jesus experienced exactly this. They were transformed not by what they received, but by what they surrendered.

Zechariah gave up his confusion and disbelief. Joseph gave up his fear and conflicted feelings. Mary surrendered her whole self—body, mind, and heart. The shepherds gave their joyous praise to God. The magi gave their most precious gifts to the baby, and then chose to turn away from Herod. The Christmas story, time and again, is about the great lengths God went to in drawing near to us, and the joyous obedience to God we are called to offer in return.

It is not about the gifts we give. It is about the gifts we become to God and to others.

And if that sounds antithetical to what the world would want us to believe about Christmas, it should. To be sure, we come awfully close to getting it right. We practice goodwill and cheer, and basically try to be decent toward others. That's good. We observe the essential practices of the Christian faith, going to worship and remembering the Christmas story. That's good, too. And we have a sincere desire to do our best for God. Good intentions are better than nothing.

But if that is all that constitutes our observance of Christmas—basic goodness, basic practices, and basic sincerity —then John Wesley, founder of the Methodist movement, would have a word to describe our efforts: *Almost.*

Wesley preached a sermon to his fellow Oxford University colleagues at St. Mary's Church on July 25, 1741, called "The Almost Christian," in which he described a person who, on the surface, had all the outward appearances of godliness. This person did all the basic things right: practiced decency toward others, went to church, abstained from bad behavior, and sincerely tried to do his best. But Wesley would say that as commendable as that person might be (and wouldn't it be great if everyone were at least that good), he would only be almost a Christian. If all of these good things and more characterized our lives, Wesley would stand before us today, hold a mirror to our souls, and in his best Dennis the Menace impression, say to us: "Is that all?"

He would say, "Is that all you've got to give God?" Doesn't God deserve more? Isn't it possible that God has given you his Spirit and empowered you to do more than just the basics, and has called you to make an extraordinary impact for the Kingdom? Doesn't God want nothing less than your whole heart?

In that same sermon, Wesley calls followers of Jesus to do more than live an "almost" life. He calls them to live an "altogether" life, one that, first of all, fully loves God: "Such a love is this," he writes, "as engrosses the whole heart, as rakes up all the affections, as fills the entire capacity of the soul and employs the utmost extent of all its faculties."[1] Second, he calls them to fully love others, including and especially those who have wronged us, and those whom we have wronged. Third, he calls them to have a full trust and confidence in God, so that faith is not just an exercise in intellectual conviction, but a holistic offering of mind, body, and spirit. An "altogether" Christian is one who unreservedly and wholeheartedly trusts God and puts that trust into action.

If this all seems formidable, then it should be. If this seems like a much taller order than just preparing for Christmas, that's because it is. But the good news is, that is what Advent is for. Despite our inclinations to skip ahead to the manger and get to Christmas as soon as possible, these four weeks of Advent are meant to recalibrate us away from merely living an almost kind of life and toward an altogether commitment to Christ.

Wesley's sermon was not intended to be an Advent or Christmas sermon, of course. In fact, we don't have record that Wesley ever preached an Advent sermon, or even formally observed Advent. This was likely due to the influence of the Puritans in eighteenth-century England, who saw Christmas as merely an appropriation of a pagan holiday. We know from his journals that Wesley acknowledged Christmas and even preached sermons on that day. But we don't know that he ever observed Advent.

But even though "The Almost Christian" wasn't essentially an Advent message, it can still give us guidance on how to be prepared for Christmas, especially for preparing to receive Christ more fully in our hearts and lives. Consider the following questions, drawn straight from this sermon, as a way of asking how we can be a gift to God this Advent. You might even choose to use these questions as a personal spiritual Advent calendar, praying through one question every day from now until Christmas:

1. Do I so far practice justice, mercy, and truth, as even the world requires?
2. Do I even appear on the outside to be a Christian?
3. Do I practice godly behavior?
4. Do I refrain from doing evil things, as is described in the Bible?
5. Do I do good with all my might?
6. Do I seriously follow God's commandments whenever I can?
7. Do I do everything with a sincere plan and desire to please God in every way?
8. Am I, at the very least, observing the qualities of an "almost" Christian?
9. Am I willing to go a step further and be an "altogether" Christian?
10. Is the love of God shed abroad in my heart?
11. Can I cry out, "My God, and my All"?
12. Do I desire nothing but God?
13. Am I happy in God?

14. Is God my glory, my delight, and my source of joy?

15. Is this commandment written in my heart: "That he who loves God loves others also?"

16. Do I love my neighbor as myself?

17. Do I love everyone, even my enemies, even the enemies of God, as my own soul?

18. Do I love others as Christ loved me?

19. Do I believe that Christ loved me and gave himself for me?

20. Do I have faith in Christ's blood?

21. Do I believe that Jesus has taken away my sins and cast them as a stone into the depth of the sea?

22. Do I believe that Jesus has blotted out the handwriting that was against me, taking it out of the way, nailing it to his cross?

23. Do I feel the assurance that I have been redeemed of my sins?

24. Do I feel the assurance of the Spirit that I am a child of God?

25. And the last question, based on Wesley's final instruction is: Can I lift my hand up to heaven, and declare to him that lives forever and ever, "Lord, You know all things. You know that I love You"?

Ultimately, Wesley concludes this sermon with a paragraph that very well could summarize our hope for what this Advent, this season of being "almost Christmas," might mean for you:

> May we all thus experience what it is to be, not almost only; but altogether Christians; being justified freely by his grace, through the redemption that is in Jesus; knowing we have peace with God through Jesus Christ; rejoicing in hope of the glory of God; and having the love of God shed abroad in our hearts, by the Holy Ghost given unto us![2]

Notice, first of all, that he calls us to *experience* what an altogether commitment might look like. That's why we have subtitled this study "A Wesleyan Advent *Experience*." It is our hope that you will make Advent this year more than just an intellectual acknowledgment of what this season means, or by simply treating these exercises as mere responsibilities to check off among many during this busy time. To make this an experience requires making your spiritual maturity and commitment a priority, with your full focus and all your faculties of mind, body, heart, and spirit, just as the Great Commandment requires us.

Second, notice the choice language that Wesley uses in this last paragraph (emphasis added):

"... knowing we have *peace* with God through Jesus Christ,"
"... *rejoicing* in *hope* of the glory of God,"
"... and having the *love* of God shed abroad in our hearts."

Peace. Joy. Hope. Love.

No, this was not an Advent sermon. But it underscores the four qualities that we most attribute to Advent; and fully living out these ideals can not only be the marks of an altogether Christian, it can lead us to an altogether Christmas.

So, for the next four weeks, we will explore each of these words more fully. We'll delve into the Scriptures, share some stories from our own experience, tap into more of John Wesley's thoughts and writings, and include some of Charles Wesley's beautiful hymns. And, we'll conclude with a call to covenant renewal, a hallmark of the Wesleyan faith, and a perfect way to "lift our hand up to heaven" and say, "My Lord, and My God!"

We'll do all of this, not by our own power and strength, but by "the Holy Ghost given unto us."

So, welcome to Advent.

Let's become a gift to God and one another.

And let's experience an altogether Christmas.

CHAPTER 1

AN ALTOGETHER *Peace*

MAGREY R. DEVEGA

Imagine you're going on a lengthy car trip on the interstate. After many long hours behind the wheel, you first see a sign that shows the name of your destination and how many more miles until you get there.

Seeing for the first time that sign with your destination and distance always feels like a twofold message. First, it's good news. It reminds you that every passing mile gets you that much closer to your arrival. Your destination is coming. But it's also sobering news. You aren't there yet. You may be closer now than when you started, but you've still got a way to go. Your back is achy and your tummy is grumbling and your mind is getting numb from the seemingly endless roads you've covered, but you're still not there.

This is the tension we face every Advent season. We speak

of a Jesus who is coming again to be among us, even though we know he is already here. We speak of the presence of "peace on earth, goodwill to all," though the evidence around us feels like it is a long way from coming. Even though society sings of it as "the most wonderful time of the year," we know that the distance to that destination feels very far indeed.

So every Advent, we have destination and distance signs on the road to the manger. They say *peace*, *hope*, *love*, and *joy*. With every passing Sunday, we might have the same response: our destination is coming, but boy, oh boy, we have a long way to go. Each week is a reminder that we have *almost* attained these things, but we aren't there yet.

An "almost hope" reminds us that there are brighter days ahead, but we still have to go through the darkness. And it's hard to go through those times.

An "almost love" reminds us that the world is filled with lots of synthetic, temporary definitions of love. And none of them are as fulfilling as the love that God desires for us and from us.

An "almost joy" points to a God who can meet our deepest needs with an everlasting contentment. But in the meantime, we wrestle with fleeting, unsatisfying fillers.

The chapters ahead will take us to some pretty deep places showing us how to claim the arrival of a God-with-us, who sees us through to the destination regardless of how long we have traveled, or how long it feels before we get there. It will help us cover the distance between *almost* and *altogether*.

And in this chapter, we see this destination and distance sign: "Almost Peace."

It doesn't take much to realize how many miles we have to go before we get to the destination of an altogether peace. Just read the news headlines about the latest flare-up in another troubled spot in the world. Think about violence and war going on between many nations and people groups, or the damage we are doing to the planet itself. Think about the harm we cause one another in this country, not just with our actions but with our rhetoric and prejudice as well. Think about the broken relationships you have with loved ones and friends, and the layers of bitterness, betrayal, and heartache that you've seen over the miles.

And think about the lack of peace within your own heart. About the unsettledness you feel about your future, the conflict you have against your own inner demons of guilt and shame, and the inability you have to tame the wild horses of anger, fear, and powerlessness.

Yes, peace seems miles away.

Oh, we do our best to project an "almost peace." Wesley used that term "almost" to describe the Christian who had the outward "form of godliness," but still fell short of "altogether" godliness on the inside. We cover up our insecurities, we put on a good face amid chaos to convince others—and even ourselves—that things are better than they are. But on the inside, deep down inside, we are far from peaceful. We might even be afraid.

It should be no wonder that each of the characters in Jesus' birth narrative had very similar struggles. The Gospels would want to remind us that none of Jesus' closest family and associates had perfect, trouble-free lives when he was born. That's why, for each of them, the angels' first message was "Don't be afraid."

The first character that Luke introduces to us in his birth narrative was Zechariah, the old childless priest who was visited by the angel (Luke 1:5-25). And when Gabriel brought him some amazing news, Luke says he was "startled and overcome with fear" (1:12). He was in need of peace.

Later, we meet Mary, the young, unwed girl, who was initially troubled by the appearance of the angel Gabriel (Luke 1:26-38). She wrestled with how to deal with the news that she would be bearing a child. Not just any child, but the very Son of God himself. To Mary, just as to Zechariah, Gabriel gave reassurance with the words "Don't be afraid."

Then, when Jesus was born, there were those shepherds out in the fields (Luke 2:8-20). And when their night sky was emblazoned with a fireworks display of singing angels, they weren't just afraid; they were terrified. They too were in need of peace, which the angels had come to proclaim. "Don't be afraid," the angel tells them (Luke 2:10).

Skip over to Matthew, and there is a lack of peace everywhere. There we meet Joseph, who was so troubled upon hearing the news that Mary was pregnant that the angel had to encourage him to hang in there (Matthew 1:18-25). Yes, your fiancée is pregnant, and yes, it is not your child, and yes, the law says you should send her away. But don't leave her, Joseph. You can bet that Joseph was in need of peace in his heart.

And then, of course, there was Herod, who was the epitome

of all that is contrary to peace. When he found out about the birth of Jesus, he was terrified, jealous, paranoid, and dead set on finding the child and snuffing him out (Matthew 2:1-16). Were it not for the angel warning Joseph in a dream to flee to Egypt with Jesus and Mary, Herod would have had his way.

Over and over again in the Gospels, we are reminded that the world Jesus entered was one that needed a whole lot of peace. Not just in society and in relationships, but deep within the human heart.

I would think you've had moments when you have needed peace within yourself.

I sure have.

Peace: Anger's Antidote

I don't know what it is about the holidays, but they tend to amplify the ongoing chaos in our lives—especially when it comes to our relationships with loved ones. Sometimes, that heightened tension bubbles up to the point that we exhibit characteristics we would much rather pretend we didn't have, like our capacity to be angry.

I won't soon forget the time not long ago when I discovered my own capacity to be angry while in a tense situation with loved ones. I was frustrated with so much stress in my life, with mounting pressures at home and at work, that one day I blew up in front of my two teenage daughters. They had not cleaned their rooms as I had been asking them to do. Granted, they were busy with their own school pressures, and they were trying to get all their homework done, but they still hadn't done it.

I grew angry, and I just blew up at them. I yelled in a way that I rarely yell, an at-the-top-of-my-lungs kind of yell. I'm glad, in retrospect, that they looked so surprised at me in that moment, as if it was rare that they ever saw this side of me. Frankly, I was even more surprised than they were, as I had forgotten that I had the capability to express that level of anger.

Anger can be scary. When it erupts inside you, like a wild beast, it can feel uncontrollable.

The Bible gives plenty of practical advice when it comes to finding peace amid your anger. In a text from Ephesians, which we will explore more fully later, Paul tells Christians to be angry, but not to sin (Ephesians 4:26). It's helpful to note that anger is not, in and of itself, sinful. Frustration is a natural part of life. If you've been hurt, it's natural to be angry. If you see injustice, anger is appropriate. If you are frustrated with yourself, anger happens.

True peace, as Martin Luther King Jr. once said, "is not merely the absence of tensions, but . . . the presence of . . . justice."[1] So, the better question is not "How can I avoid feeling angry?" Nor is it "How can I repress these angry feelings?" The better question is "How can I find a peace that transforms my anger into something healthy, productive, and life-giving for myself and for others?"

Think about following these three steps:

Awareness

It's important first to think about where anger comes from. Moral philosopher Martha Nussbaum suggests that the source

18

of anger is a fear that is fed by powerlessness.[2] So, the next time you feel angry, ask yourself, "What is it that I am afraid of in this situation? Why do I feel so powerless? And am I really as powerless as I think I am?"

Acceptance

Second, accept the anger that you feel. The worst thing you can do is try to repress or hide your anger, to tuck it deep down inside and pretend it's not there. You know full well that those feelings do not just disappear. If you try to ignore those feelings, they will eventually affect you physically, emotionally, and relationally. I heard of one person who was so angry at the betrayal of a friend that whenever he was in the presence of that friend, he would suffer from nosebleeds. Repressing anger, or feeling guilty about that anger, is not the answer.

Action

The toughest part of feeling angry, of course, is knowing what to do with anger. How can you take action in a way that is healthy and life-giving rather than destructive? Paul says, "Don't let the sun set on your anger" (Ephesians 4:26). In other words, don't sit there and do nothing about it. Take some action. Be proactive.

Why? Well, Paul puts it pretty clearly in the next verse: "Don't provide an opportunity for the devil" (Ephesians 4:27). Leaving anger unresolved leaves room for the devil. Remember that another name for the devil is *tempter*. Unresolved anger creates opportunities for temptations to blossom and fester, and it can lead to harmful, debilitating consequences. Resolving anger by taking healthy action removes the possibility for those temptations.

In the wake of my own anger, I took action. Several minutes after I blew up at the girls, I came in to apologize. It's not easy for a parent to apologize to a child. But I had to. I'm not sure I said all the right things, but I did my best. I named what I was afraid of in everything I was dealing with. I acknowledged how powerless I was. I said I shouldn't have acted that way.

They listened, they understood.

And then I said, gently, "Now, please go clean your room."

If you find yourself in a state of tension and stress in your relationship with loved ones, especially during the chaos of the holidays, if your efforts to project an "almost peace" crumble as the anger inside you bubbles up, then you might try following the steps of awareness, acceptance, and action as well.

You and I would also do well to follow some wise words from John Wesley.

Wesley: Do Good

He was no stranger to stress, quarrels, or even anger himself. But he was very clear about the need to be a peacemaker. In his sermon "Upon Our Lord's Sermon on the Mount," John Wesley unpacked the Beatitude "Blessed are the peacemakers" by offering a plainspoken, no-nonsense definition of what it means to be a peacemaker:

But in the full extent of the word, a peace-maker is one that, as he hath opportunity, "doth good unto all men;" one that, being filled with the love of God and of all mankind, cannot confine the expressions of it to his own family, or friends, or acquaintance, or party, or to those of his own opinions;—no, nor those who are partakers of like precious faith; but steps over all these narrow bounds, that he may do good to every man, that he may, some way or other, manifest his love to neighbours and strangers, friends and enemies. He doth good to them all, as he hath opportunity, that is, on every possible occasion; "redeeming the time," in order thereto; "buying up every opportunity, improving every hour, losing no moment wherein he may profit another."[3]

Wesley's understanding of what it means to be a peacemaker may be summed up in two words: "Do good."

Wesley understood that it is easy to do good to those with whom you agree, in those relationships where there is no conflict. The real call of God is to cross the boundaries that divide you from someone else. Whether those conflicts are born out of betrayal in your relationship, or disagreements over politics or religion, or differences in race, gender, age, or any of a number of barriers, we are called to *do good*. Not just once, in the hopes that it will be enough. And not with the expectation that the other person will reciprocate in kind.

Peacemakers do good all the time, in every way.

He does good, not of one particular kind, but good in general, in every possible way; employing herein all his talents of every kind, all his powers and faculties of body and soul, all his fortune, his interest, his reputation; desiring only, that when his Lord cometh he may say, "Well done, good and faithful servant!"[4]

This is a challenge, to be sure. But Wesley believed that an altogether peace can only come when we commit to doing good all the time, in every way, with all that we have, until the very end. The primary action for anyone who wants to live an altogether peace is simply to do good.

It was a command that Jesus took seriously, and wanted to make sure his disciples understood fully.

Just look at what he says in John 14.

John 14: Peace, Not as the World Gives

The way John tells the story, Jesus must have been powered by Red Bull or something when he was speaking here. That's what I would have needed if I were going to speak for as long as he did in this section of the Gospels. From John 13 to 16—three and a half chapters—Jesus spoke to his disciples, uninterrupted except for the questions his disciples were asking. That's over 150 verses, which is one of the longest collections of teachings and sayings of Jesus, even longer than the Sermon on the Mount.

And it couldn't come at a more critical time. This is Jesus downloading his final set of instructions and encouragement to his disciples in the final hours of his life. Moments before his arrest and death, he was telling the disciples the most important things he would want them to remember when he was gone, much of which could be summarized with five words, in John 14:27: "Peace I leave with you."

In fact, this speech ends with more words about peace: "I've said these things to you so that you will have peace in me. In the world you have distress. But be encouraged! I have conquered the world" (John 16:33). After this Jesus prayed to God, then went to the garden where he would be betrayed and arrested.

Peace was his last gift to his disciples before he died.

Yes, this is an Advent journey. And it might seem strange to hear a story from the end of Jesus' life right as we are preparing for the beginning of it. But if we pan the camera out wide and take in the whole of Jesus' life, what we discover is that from the beginning until the end, this has been a recurring, connecting thread: Jesus came to bring peace. He was born into a world that needed peace. He lived in a world that needed peace. And he was leaving behind a world that would need to know peace.

We remember that the world Jesus lived in had a very different understanding of what peace looked like. For the ancient Roman world, peace came through power. Roman peace (or *pax romana*, as it is often known) emerged about thirty years before Jesus, after centuries of war as Roman rulers extended the territorial expanse of the empire. On the surface, Roman peace may have had an absence of war, but it was not the kind of peace that Martin Luther King Jr. preached about. It was not peace found by the presence of justice, or equality, or wholeness of all of life. It was a peace that was forged by the oppression of all who would rise up against imperial Rome. Political and military opponents were beaten down and stripped of their ability to rise up in resistance. It was a peace embodied by the horrors of King Herod, Roman ruler of Judea at the time of Jesus' birth. Upon receiving word of Jesus' birth, Herod perceived him to be a threat and attempted to kill him to preserve the peace.

This was the definition of peace at the time of Jesus. So, when he made his final plea to his disciples on the night before he died, he told them that the peace he was leaving them was not like Roman peace. "My peace I give you. I give to you not as the world gives" (John 14:27). Jesus' peace would not be sustained by fear or oppression. It would not be born of anger or revenge. This peace would not be through the accumulation of power.

It would be born of love.

Shalom

Jesus' idea of peace would have been an understanding derived from the Hebrew word *shalom*, which we often translate as "peace." It's really one of the most important words in the entire Bible. And like most Hebrew words, our English language doesn't have a word that fully captures its nuances.

Unlike our word *peace*, which can simply mean an absence of conflict or war, or a feeling of serenity or contentment, the definition of *shalom* is much bigger and more comprehensive.

Shalom comes from the root word *shalam*, which means "to be completed," "to be healthy or uninjured," or "to keep peace."

It means peace but also speaks of wholeness, completeness, and fullness. If we look at the broad biblical witness, we find that shalom often envisions the whole and complete restoration of all creation.

In other words, this kind of peace starts with a wholeness in yourself, but it does not stop there. It then offers wholeness in your relationships with others. Then, as more relationships are restored, we can have shalom communities and eventually a shalom world. Shalom doesn't just mean the absence of conflict or trouble. It points to the fullness of health and prosperity for oneself and others.

So, for three and a half chapters in John's Gospel, for 150 verses, Jesus was conferring that kind of peace—shalom—upon his disciples and upon us.

But Jesus even goes one step further than that. Notice, in John 14:27, what I think is one of the most important words in this entire passage. He says, "Peace I leave with you. *My* peace I give to you" (emphasis added).

Jesus isn't just wishing them peace. He isn't just offering a blessing for peace. He isn't simply saying "I'm giving you some sentiment of peace." He said, "*My* peace I give to you." He is offering a part of himself. He is leaving them a part of who he is as a way to help them through their troubled times.

Think about what that would have meant to those disciples —those people who, for three and a half years, would have witnessed Jesus demonstrate some remarkable abilities for peace.

That same Jesus was able to sleep on a boat in the middle of a storm. He showed these disciples how to be calm amid the storms of life and how to settle the waves and wind with just a single word. He was giving them *that* peace from within himself.

That same Jesus was able to stand up to those who were finding fault with him, challenging him in public, and seeking to undermine everything he was trying to do for good. He showed them how to speak up without shame, to walk through the crowds without fear, to stand up for what was right, and even to forgive his tormentors as he was on the cross. He was giving them *that* peace from within himself.

That same Jesus was able to stare death squarely in the eye at the graveside of Lazarus and at the bedside of Jairus's daughter. He spoke a word of comfort to the grieving and a word of hope about the Resurrection. Jesus was giving them that kind of peace, that ability to name your grief and acknowledge your loss, and to know that death is not the final word.

That same Jesus drew together, shaped, and empowered a group of ragtag disciples, drawn from all walks of life, from various political perspectives, who were often at one another's throats with competition and one-upmanship: Matthew the conservative, Peter the liberal, and every type of person in between. He was giving them *that* kind of peace, that ability to unite together on the one thing that mattered most: serving one another in love.

And do you know what? Jesus is giving you *that* same kind of peace as well.

Yes, that may seem hard for you right now. When you look in the mirror, you may see anything but shalom. The wrinkles and furrows on your brow represent years of hardship and heartache. The look in your eyes reveals the endless disagreements you have with people about controversial issues. The frown on your face indicates the fractured nature of our relationships and our society.

But the message of the angels to Zechariah, Mary, Joseph, and the shepherds is all the same for you: Do not fear. Do not be afraid.

Why? Because Jesus has given you a part of himself, a piece of his peace.

Later in John's Gospel, just a few chapters later, after Jesus' death, the resurrected Jesus appeared to his disciples, in John 20:19. And what do you suppose was the first thing he said to them after he was resurrected? Well, it's exactly the same as the last thing he said before he died: "Peace be with you." He then goes on:

> Jesus said to them again, "Peace be with you. As the
> Father sent me, so I am sending you." Then he breathed
> on them and said, "Receive the Holy Spirit. If you
> forgive anyone's sins, they are forgiven; if you don't
> forgive them, they aren't forgiven." (John 20:21-23)

It's almost as if he was picking up exactly where he left off three days prior—still talking about peace, still giving them the part of himself that would enable them to live without fear. Just like Zechariah, and Mary, and Joseph, and the shepherds learned to live.

And it is the same *shalom* that Jesus is breathing upon you today.

Ephesians 4: Maintaining Unity of the Spirit in the Bond of Peace

It feels incongruous to see the word *peace* emblazoned on our holiday decorations and Christmas cards in a culture that seems so divided and polarized. Yet we remember that the world into which Jesus was born was not one of harmony, mutuality, and "goodwill to all," but one fractured by mistrust between people in power and oppressed people in the margins—a world not unlike our own.

The Apostle Paul offers some helpful guidance in this Advent exploration of peace in the letter he shared with the people of Ephesus.

The letter to the Ephesian church is different from every other epistle Paul wrote. Unlike the others, it doesn't address an issue that was unique to that particular ancient community, and it contains few references to individuals within that church. In other words, much of what Paul says to the Ephesian church can be generally applied to every congregation. He could just as easily be writing to the Christians today as he did to those early Christians two thousand years ago.

Paul's words to the Ephesians address the need for unity—something we still wrestle with today. Christians in Paul's time as well as our own experience the tension between honoring our differences and looking for commonalities. It's a tension between recognizing our differences as something to celebrate rather than minimalize, and emphasizing our commonalities that draw us together. It's the need in community to find common ground without coercing people into boxes they don't belong in.

For first-century Christians as well as for us, tribalism is a comfortable mindset to fall into. It's easy to draw lines between insiders and outsiders, and to think of ourselves as the insiders. I do it as much as anybody else. First-century Christians felt discord between Jews and Gentiles. We may no longer line up according to those same boundaries, but you can bet we are still tribalists at heart. Left vs. Right, Liberal vs. Conservative, Citizen vs. Immigrant, Educated vs. Less Educated, Urban vs. Rural—we experience disagreements over abortion, immigration, the death penalty, racial and gender discrimination, and the role of government.

But here is what Ephesians can teach us. Even though unity is a lot easier when there is uniformity, unity from diversity is a lot closer to the heart of God.

Paul's Letter to the Ephesians reminds us that the heart of God calls us to focus on what we can all be for, rather than what we might be against. Read how Paul calls us to remember what ought to hold us together in common in Ephesians 4:3-6:

> Make an effort to preserve the unity of the Spirit with the peace that ties you together. You are one body and one spirit, just as God also called you in one hope. There is one Lord, one faith, one baptism, and one God and Father of all, who is over all, through all, and in all.

That word *one* is like a pulse in this passage. It reflects the oneness that is in the heartbeat of God. Celebrate our diversity. Honor our differences. And at the end of the day, work toward unity together.

So, how do we do that? Well, Paul gives us some very practical guidance on how to be peacemakers in a time of cultural discord. He shows us how to "maintain the unity of the Spirit in the bond of peace" (Ephesians 4:3 NRSV).

In Ephesians 4:25-32, there is a list of seven practical instructions. Paul intended these to guide the Ephesians in living in unity with one another and with Christ. We can use them to relate in a Christlike way to someone we have strong disagreements with. This guidance is especially helpful during holiday family gatherings, when differences of opinion can be most put on display. Whatever those controversial topics might be, consider the following advice from Paul:

1. *Speak truth.* Paul says in verse 25, "*Each of you must tell the truth to your neighbor.*" When you are sharing information, whether it is in person, or especially on social media, make sure the facts are straight. Be open to the possibility that the facts may be against you. And don't spread lies.

2. *Watch your anger.* Paul says in verse 26, "*Be angry without sinning.*" He does not say don't be angry; he says be angry without sinning—that is, be angry in a way that does not destroy the humanity of another person or disobey God.

3. *Don't steal* (someone else's dignity). Paul says in verse 28, "Thieves should no longer steal. Instead, they should go to work, using their hands to do good." Though Paul was referring to stealing property, we can apply his words also to the dignity that belongs to someone else. And in the context of polarized debate, the worst thing you can steal is someone else's dignity. As Bishop Gregory Palmer has said, "If my sense of self-worth comes at the expense of your self-worth, I'm doing it wrong."[5] Instead, use your words and actions to do good.

4. *Practice empathy.* Paul says in verse 28, "do good so that [you] will have something to share with whoever is in need." Remember that all of us have needs. You are not the only one. Discover the woundedness and hurt in another person's eyes, and you will discover that you may not only have the means to bring them healing, you will also find healing for yourself.

5. *Watch your language.* Verse 29: "Don't let any foul words come out of your mouth. Only say what is helpful when it is needed for building up the community so that it benefits those who hear what you say." This one is pretty self-explanatory. May the purpose of your conversations be to find understanding, not to score points; build up, don't tear down.

6. *Guard your heart.* Verse 31: "Put aside all bitterness, losing your temper, anger, shouting, and slander, along with every other evil." Do you know what? It doesn't

matter how holy your behavior is if it isn't motivated out of a heart of peace. Get rid of anything in your life that is not love.

7. *Be kind, compassionate, and forgiving.* Verse 32: "Be kind, compassionate, and forgiving to each other, in the same way God forgave you in Christ." These last two are pretty straightforward. Kindness and compassion are godly virtues. And every time you forgive or ask for forgiveness, you participate in God's comprehensive restoration of the whole broken world. It is that important.

The next time you get caught up in a polarizing discussion, whether it be at the holiday dinner table, or at the next Christmas party, or even on social media, speak the truth and work toward peace.

Paul is so passionate about getting this right. Why? Because he believes that if the church gets it right, then the world can get it right. If followers of Jesus can model a different way to seek unity amid our diversity, then maybe the world can discover a better way. And maybe we can discover peace—real, altogether peace—amid our conflict.

Heavenly Peace

In 1818, there lived a German priest named Joseph Mohr, who pastored St. Nicholas parish in Obendorf. River flooding had damaged the church's organ that year, and so the congregation didn't have a way to play music on Christmas Eve.

What to do without an organ to lead the Christmas Eve singing? Mohr was undeterred. He pulled out a poem he had written several years before about the birth of Jesus on the first Christmas and took it to Franz Gruber, the schoolmaster and organist of a nearby town. He asked Gruber to write a simple melody for his poem that could be played on guitar. In several hours, Gruber had the music done and the carol was played for the first time at the Christmas Eve service.

That poem, that carol, was titled "Stille Nacht." "Silent Night."

Fast-forward almost one hundred years later, to 1914. Still on Christmas Eve, still in Europe, but this time a very different setting. In the trenches of World War I, in northern France, stood battalions of British soldiers staring down their German counterparts, engaged in brutal battle.

Among them was nineteen-year-old Charles Brewer, a British lieutenant, shivering with his fellow soldiers. They had been at war for five months, one million lives had been taken, and there was no end to the war in sight.

As Brewer recalled the story, something amazing then happened. A British sentry suddenly spied a glistening light on the German parapet, less than one hundred yards away. Warned that it might be a trap, Brewer slowly raised his head over the soaked sandbags. Through the maze of barbed wire, he saw a sparkling Christmas tree.

Brewer then noticed the rising of a faint sound that he had never before heard on the battlefield. Singing. In German.

The words of "Stille Nacht." The words were unfamiliar to the British soldiers, but the melody certainly wasn't.

When the Germans finished singing, the Brits erupted with applause. And instead of returning fire, they returned in song, singing the English version of that hymn.

When dawn broke on Christmas morning, something even more remarkable happened. In sporadic pockets along the five-hundred–mile Western Front, unarmed German and Allied soldiers tentatively emerged from the trenches and cautiously crossed no-man's-land to exchange small gifts and to wish each other a Merry Christmas.

This hymn, and other gestures of goodwill, succeeded where political and military officials had failed to bring a cease-fire in the war. Likewise, a hymn that speaks about silence amid our noise and busyness, and heavenly peace amid the tumult of war, speaks to all of us today.

British Corporal John Ferguson said, "We shook hands, wished each other a Merry Xmas and were soon conversing as if we had known each other for years. . . . Here we were laughing and chatting to men whom only a few hours before we were trying to kill!"[6]

This Christmas Eve, you will likely be singing that hymn as part of your celebration of the birth of Christ. When you do, may its words and melody be an invitation to silence your very noisy soul. Find in this baby Jesus a calm, contentment, and joy that only God can bring you.

That you might sleep in heavenly peace.

An Altogether Peace

Ultimately, living an altogether peace transforms lives and relationships, and eventually the entire world. At the end of John Wesley's sermon on Matthew 5, he described the hope and possibility of a world in which God's people learn to be conduits of peace:

> [Being a peacemaker] implies those lovers of God and man who utterly detest and abhor all strife and debate, all variance and contention; and accordingly labour with all their might, either to prevent this fire of hell from being kindled, or, when it is kindled, from breaking out, or, when it is broke out, from spreading any farther. They endeavour to calm the stormy spirits of men, to quiet their turbulent passions, to soften the minds of contending parties, and, if possible, reconcile them to each other. They use all innocent arts, and employ all their strength, all the talents which God has given them, as well to preserve peace where it is, as to restore it where it is not.[7]

Advent is a time of longing and preparation for Jesus to come, though we acknowledge that Jesus is already among us. So it is with peace. We look at the world around us, and the conflict among us, and we feel like the advent of peace is a long way away. But the possibility of peace is already here. It is found in the presence of God and the power of the Holy Spirit, to help us embody the peace that only Christ can bring.

Questions for Reflection

1. What kind of peace do you long for?

2. How might you begin to seek shalom within yourself? with another person? for the world?

3. Which of Paul's practical instructions for peacemaking are hardest for you? What can you do to begin practicing them regularly?

Hymn Reflection

"Thou Hidden Source of Calm Repose"
(*The United Methodist Hymnal*, 153)

The word *peace* has two related, but not identical, uses. One denotes the peace that comes between communities. In its fullest sense, this peace is both the absence of war and the presence of justice. The other meaning of the word is an inward personal peace. This peace is synonymous with calm, tranquility, and serenity. In Advent, as we each prepare for the coming again of the Christ Child, we seek to gain and understand this personal and inward peace even as we long for communal peace.

Charles Wesley's hymn "Thou Hidden Source of Calm Repose" elucidates the praise we have for Jesus who is the ultimate source of inward peace. First published in the 1749 *Hymns and Sacred Poems*, it appears as the thirty-first of forty-three hymns in the section "Hymns for Believers." Though it does not contain a direct Advent theme of waiting for the coming Christ Child, it does offer an example of what faith in Jesus can provide.

The text starts with a description of how Jesus acts in the life of the believer, saying in essence, "You are a hidden source of calm, of ultimate love, of sanctuary from enemies, of security, and in your name I can hide from grief and shame and sin." The second verse riffs on the idea of the strength of Jesus' name: "Your name brings salvation, keeps my soul happy, brings comfort, power, peace, joy, love, pardon, holiness and heaven."

The third verse continues this theme of the power of Jesus'

name, but in the second line, starts a series of oppositions: rest/toil, ease/pain, healing/broken heart, war/peace, loss/gain, smile/tyrant's frown, shame/glory. The pattern continues into the fourth verse: want/plentiful supply, weakness/power, bonds/liberty, light/Satan's darkness, grief/joy, life/death, heaven/hell. It is important to note that the texts always use the singular possessive pronoun "my." This is most certainly not defining a communal calm, but a personal calm that comes from faith.

When John Wesley speaks of "knowing we have peace with God through Jesus Christ," it is in these dualities that we can see moving from an almost peace to an altogether peace. For both John and Charles, Jesus resides on the better side of these dualities, and therefore, Jesus is the ultimate peace of our souls.

CHAPTER 2

AN ALTOGETHER *H*OPE

INGRID MCINTYRE

Hope was an important part of my childhood. I'm a preacher's kid, and itinerating was part of the job description. I was a team player (mostly), but the constant possibility of moving wasn't my favorite perk. Year after year, every spring when the appointments were being set, I would shove my fear down deep and hold on to hope that this year we wouldn't have to move. The real hope was that one day I would never have to move again.

The anxiety and suspicion that rose in me every time moving day came around made places like my granny's cozy high-rise, my grandaddy's farm tucked in the hollow, and my cousin's saltbox house in a Norman Rockwell-esque town feel like magical places of safety and sameness. These locations represented hope to me. They seemed to remain unchanged over time, something foreign to me as I experienced a full-on fruit-basket-turnover every five to six years.

This hope blossomed every Christmas when I visited them. The same was true for spring breaks, Thanksgiving, Easter, and the occasional long weekend here and there . . . I felt such comfort and excitement every time one of these family members welcomed me into their home after the long drive we sometimes referred to as "Six Sesame Streets." Particularly during the years when we were appointed to move and my anxiety was extra high, or after we had just recently moved and beginning again felt impossible, their homes were places I could count on to be the same as they were the last time I visited. I could find my games in the same drawer, we all sat around the same table with the same pictures hanging on the same walls, and we were always fixing the same piece of weak fencing where the calves escaped into the same angry neighbor's yard. Ah, stability.

Their homes were places, and they were people, that brought me hope in the midst of change. Their consistency was my comfort when I was unsettled and in the midst of my own personal chaos and despair. I fit with them. My hope took the shape of knowing that there was a familiar place I could go—always. I remember thinking, "I hope I can have a home that never changes one day."

I usually had a countdown between visits made of construction paper links. I guess it's the only thing that would help with my lack of patience. When the last link was torn, the countdown was over and the day *finally* arrived to depart for one of these havens of hope. I would shake off any feelings of *almost* belonging at the parsonage door, pack my bags for the familiar destination, and willingly (mostly) stay on my side of the car until we arrived. And then there we were, where I knew I belonged and was welcomed with great love and celebration. I never questioned or wondered how this scenario would play out. What a gift.

This was a hope of my childhood. I held on to that hope that I could disappear into a safe, loving space that was familiar, even if it was just a few days. Knowing my people were out there and loved me made slogging through some of the changes we went through as a family tolerable.

Yet looking back, I see that this hope of my childhood was an "almost hope," not because it was inadequate or only partly hopeful, but because it only focused on me. I understand now that not everyone has such a family or community to walk alongside them in the journey or to greet them with love upon arrival. When I realized that I was going to be a part of the whole family of Christ, I realized what an altogether hope would require. It would require expanding my hope to include looking forward to the well-being of others. Such a hope would mean me stretching as a Christian, and it wasn't always going to feel good. My family was not just my mom and dad and brother anymore. It was the world. And a lot of it looked different from me. If I was going to be a part of it and a part of the hope that we all so desperately desire, I was going to have to push through with a lot of help from God. Altogether hope means embracing struggle, leaning on God, and looking forward to the well-being of others.

Wesley: Birthing Hope

John Wesley was a tangible hope-bearer to the people in England who were oppressed by the inequities of their kingdom. He was an agent of altogether hope. He witnessed pain all around him, but instead of going to the king or queen, he went directly to those who suffered right where they were—in the streets and fields. When he and his brother Charles faced challenges from naysayers and institutions, they persevered. Who were these guys? Radicals! (I bet there wasn't liability insurance back then.)

Wesley didn't say, "Come to us in our big church! Bring a dish for our potluck!" Wesley did what God always does—he showed up and brought hope to the people! It's just like God tells us, "I'm going to come to *you*! And here I am—Jesus!" It wasn't about showing up to the potluck or the fancy church with the beautiful windows (though they are so beautiful) or being clean and dressing nicely. These folks were simply trying to survive, so instead, he carried hope to them. This is the difference between almost hope and altogether hope. One stands at a distance while the other relentlessly pursues; one offers platitudes while the other dives deep into the hopelessness of a situation and offers light in the darkness—light that grows and grows and grows.

People living in poverty often don't have time or the luxury to go take showers and get fancy for church. They don't have enough to feed their own families, so how could they bring food to a potluck? They don't have transportation, so how are they going to get to the church? In contrast, God tells us to "go!" This is what hope looks like close-up. We carry it with us. The hope of Christ moves through us so that he is born again and again in every moment of every day. In *every* moment of *every* day . . . not just Sundays.

None of this altogether hope is easy. None of it. Each time hope is carried to those who are struggling, our hands get dirty. Our hearts get overwhelmed. We enter unfamiliar spaces knowing it would be much easier to have stayed home.

In "The Marks of the New Birth," John Wesley wrote: "Thus St. Peter, speaking to all the children of God who were then scattered abroad, saith, 'Blessed be the God and Father of our Lord Jesus Christ, which, according to his abundant mercy, hath begotten us again unto a lively hope'. (1 Peter 1:3.)"[1]

Yes! God brings this *lively* hope to *all* of God's children no matter where they are. God breathes new life and hope into us so that hope becomes something people don't have to just be told about; they can actually see it.

Dorothy Day stands out as a great example of what hope looks like in real life. She was bold in her faith and in her life, and not perfect by any stretch of the imagination. Because of that, she's more relatable than other examples. She had love toward and with those who were marginalized, simply walking alongside them and being a physical sign of hope. Into situations far too depressing for many others to enter, she went as a hope-bearer to those who may have had no hope for themselves.

She probably understood the importance of hope far better because she had experienced her own painful circumstances.

Hope comes to us when we do not even know how to begin pursuing it, often coming through people like Dorothy Day. None of it was easy for her, but through her life's challenges, her faith became even stronger. She wrote:

> Young people say, What good can one person do? What is the sense of our small effort? They cannot see that we must lay one brick at a time, take one step at a time; we can be responsible only for the one action of the present moment. But we can beg for an increase of love in our hearts that will vitalize and transform all our individual actions, and know that God will take them and multiply them, as Jesus multiplied the loaves and fishes.[2]

What a posture of hope! Life's challenges create a thin space where the real thing, hope, becomes visible. Once we've experienced it, nothing can ever take its place.

A Ragtag Team of Hopefuls

I can't imagine that Mary or Joseph felt any kind of comfort on their journey to Bethlehem. Have you ever met someone "great with child" who wanted to ride a donkey for ninety miles? I doubt it. While Israel was living in hope of the coming of a Messiah who would restore and liberate the nation from foreign oppression, I can hear Mary ask, "Are we there yet?" Her physical experience probably got in the way of the bigger spiritual picture that was unfolding in her life. If there were angels with her, could she see them? What kept her going? How long did it take her to see that God was with them all along? Did Mary have an altogether hope?

I can understand, I think, something of the kind of hope Mary must have required to keep going on the long road to Bethlehem, and on the longer road of being a young, unwed pregnant woman with a promise that her child would be the salvation of many. My journey has involved "birthing" of a different kind, but it has been hard. And that pain can often-times get in the way.

In March 2010, I decided to quit a well-paying job that I knew was definitely not my calling. I knew it when I took it, but the dollars spoke too loudly. At that point, it hadn't been long since I had finished my degree at Wesley Seminary—a place where I went seeking tools for my justice belt. I knew I wanted to work alongside people on the margins, and that well-paying job just wasn't cutting it. At the time, my brother was living in Eleuthera, an island in the Bahamas that was the perfect place to sit and listen for God. So I took a break, went there, and just listened. I stayed about a month and returned home at the end of April. I remember thinking at the end of that time, "God! You didn't even talk to me! What am I doing wrong?" Dang. Radio Silence. *Here I am, Lord!!!*"

When I got back to Nashville, I was still searching and listening. I asked my old friend Jack if he would take me to the largest homeless encampment called "Tent City" and introduce me to some of the people living there. I told him I just wanted to meet people—nothing else. He was kind and trusted me and I met some of the most amazing humans who were so generous to share their stories with me. Because of Jack, I got involved in some of the conversations around homelessness and got on a list to receive notices about what was going on within the homeless community.

There was a workshop I had promised to lead in St. Louis, Missouri, during the last week of April. On the way home, I started getting texts from my friend who was renting the downstairs apartment in my home. I remember her saying, "Nashville's getting a whole lot of rain . . . water is coming into the basement." This had never happened before. I told my roommate to bring her stuff upstairs and when I got home, we watched the news together. It's when we started seeing houses float down the interstate that I knew something crazy was happening.

The 2010 flood in Middle Tennessee devastated Nashville, damaging and destroying property and causing eleven deaths in the city alone. More than thirteen inches of rain fell during a thirty-six-hour period, and the Cumberland River, which runs through downtown, crested at twelve feet above flood stage. Sadly, yet predictably, the vulnerable in our town were among the hardest hit.

Through the list I was on to get updates about the homeless community in Nashville, I heard about a Red Cross shelter for those from Tent City who had been relocated to the gymnasium at Lipscomb University. They'd been relocated because fourteen feet of water had covered their homes. I showed up and just said, "Put me to work." There, I met the three people who would be in it for the long haul with me. In the beginning, these three didn't quite know what to make of me. Lindsey and

Jeannie had social work backgrounds and I didn't. Brett had been learning the ropes from these fierce women. It felt like I was the oddball with a church background that didn't feel as practically useful.

Then I started reaching out to the church community I had grown up with—the many who knew me from all the moving around I did as a child and young person—and they came through for us, meeting our needs along the way. My church background gave me the contacts and the skills to help people of faith see the need and inspire them to help meet it. When the city told those living at the shelter at Lipscomb it was time to leave, together we said to our new friends, "No. You can't do it. You can't go back downtown." We knew that if they went downtown, they would be lost as so many in Nashville were focused on simply repairing their own homes after the flood. To those without anywhere to go we said, "We're going to walk with you. We don't know what it's going to look like, but let's walk together."

That experience kicked off a journey for me that I'm still on to this day. What began with walking alongside our friends who were just trying to find shelter and stability morphed into forming a not-for-profit called "Open Table Nashville" with Lindsey, Jeannie, and Brett. This journey has taken many turns with unexpected joys and hardships.

As I reflect now, it all makes sense. When I first moved back to Nashville from Wesley, I knew I wanted to do something different, because being in DC, the hub of activism, and being in seminary gave me an opportunity to see an even broader scope of what love looks like in action. Something *different* usually means birthing something new, which always carries labor pains. I thought God had not been speaking to me, but really God was just telling me to rest and wait. It's a message I wasn't used to hearing. And I discovered something else too: the changes and moves I had resisted while growing up turned out to be one of my greatest assets. They had given me a church home and community I could draw on and tap into to help make a difference in people's lives—something much better than the never-changing house I hoped for as a kid.

Hope shows up even when it feels like the labor stage never ends. All the bits and pieces of life, the struggles and despair, the uncertainty and chaos—well, maybe they are the things that provide enough contrast for us to see that it was there all along—the Hope of God. The altogether hope that makes sense of it all. We just were too busy to notice.

Hope and the World Upside Down

Hope in the Advent story comes in the form of a major paradigm shift, with societal norms turned upside down. Most of these norms centered around money and power—who had them and who didn't. Hope was coming for all people, including those who didn't have money and power. And, just to make a point, God even sent the message to and through people who didn't have either.

Here was this young girl who probably didn't have much and yet she was the one bringing Jesus the Christ into the world. It was the common shepherd boys who heard the story first from the angels, not the rich and powerful who received the breaking news. It wasn't King Herod who identified signs that a new kind of king was born, it was foreign magi who did and who embraced a new story of hope. And Elizabeth, who had wanted for so long to have a child, had not just any child but *the* child who became the forerunner of Jesus, the prophet who would help lead the people to repentance and toward justice.

How ridiculous is this? Can you imagine the shepherds who saw the angels appear? They probably fell out. "Are you talking to us?" They were spoken to, and then became the ones to speak. We usually hear big proclamations through the mayor or president or other officials, and suddenly, people were listening to some ragtag shepherds. How often does that happen? Usually good news comes to and through the rich and powerful, not those living on the margins.

All of this had been in the works for a long time. None of it just happened overnight. "I know the plans I have in mind for you, declares the Lord, plans to prosper you and not to harm you, plans to give you hope and a future" (Jeremiah 29:11). Think of the generations before Mary who had held on to hope. This whole narrative gives me hope even for me . . . for your people and my people.

Hope—the real thing—breaks into seemingly strange, unexpected places where people often can't afford much of anything. When we're comfortable, can we even hear the angels? So often, people who are in some form of pain seem to hear and see much more easily. Pain often leads to hope because it *requires* hope— what else can sustain us when life is hard? This has been true for me, at least. I know that if I had I been working in my former affluent job, I would not have been looking for God the same as I do in this thin space I live in now. God takes our perceived weaknesses and uses them as our strengths. In finding homes for those living without them, God sought me because maybe I'm the only stubborn ass who would push through! Realize that altogether hope doesn't require you to put on your Sunday best. Hope—the real thing—will come when you let yourself be real. Let that be enough.

Wesley and Altogether Hope

The summer after fifth grade, I went on a trip to the British Isles with my parents. My dad is into church history, but he is a John Wesley *nerd*. So, we spent lots of time at all the John Wesley everythings. The only thing I remembered was the church in Epworth—the one he got kicked out of. Even as a kid, I thought it was incredibly faithful that Wesley didn't take no for an answer from the church, and when they wouldn't let him say the things that he felt compelled to say, he just found another place to say them in front of people who wanted to listen, who understood. From a graveyard, he gave words of life—standing on his father's grave! He didn't let power and status quo stand in his way; he went for it, putting his hope in God.

John Wesley saw and experienced the same societal problems as others, but instead of accepting them, he raised hell about them so that just maybe a few neglected others could experience hope. Life was terrible for so many people, and the Church of England wasn't living up to the church Wesley saw described in the Scriptures. *If there are so many Christians, why are people still hungry and thirsty? Why is there slavery? Why isn't Christ's presence felt in prison?* Wesley became prophetic hope for the church, speaking out boldly and making known, "Is it not hard that even those who are with us should be against us; that a man's enemies, in some degree, should be those of the same household of faith? Yet so it is."[3] Church wasn't and still isn't the building or denomination. It's Christ's body active in the world, standing outside with those who don't "belong" until a sense of belonging is experienced by all.

Wesley birthed a movement that we continue to birth today. He certainly wasn't the only one thinking the Church of England was corrupt. Other people were thinking these things too. Hope came when a group of people were unwilling to stay silent, who weren't too afraid to stand up and say, "We just can't do this anymore. We can't keep living one way at home and another way at church. The flock is not being fed, sustained, celebrated, and loved." There could and can be more!

Instead of just saying the words, "Thy kingdom come," Wesley let God embody the hope of those words through his flesh! People who didn't feel the pain of the poor and oppressed weren't so pleased with him. Why couldn't he have just stayed quiet? That rabble-rouser! If John Wesley came to a United Methodist church today, it would be interesting what he'd share with us about his experience.

Then and now, we have to be willing to show up in the strangest places, where nobody else wants to look, because that's exactly where God goes. Showing up in that way is altogether hope in action. That's exactly where Jesus is born, again and again. Those places are inside the church walls and faith traditions, *and* at homeless and refugee encampments, prisons, food pantries, protests, and political offices.

The same problems Wesley addressed are still in the world today. We're still working on prison reform, human trafficking, improvements on people's living conditions, poverty, and hunger. We get caught up in systems that marginalize others, and become complicit in those systems simply because we can't feel the pain of the poor and oppressed. Without the hope-filled prophetic voices calling us to a greater consciousness, we fail as a church.

My mother made a quilt for my nephew, and when all of those pieces were scattered on the floor, they just looked like a jumbled mess. They were different shapes and sizes and colors. None of them looked alike. Coming together, they each carried something that made the whole quilt what it needed to be to give warmth and beauty, to tell her love story for him.

I know that I am not going to end homelessness, but hope is alive in me that I can do my part and that's all God is asking. But what an amazing legacy we have to build on! What would happen if no one else was willing to "stand on a grave" and call forth the kingdom of God? Hope would diminish. Our liberation is caught up in one another's. I am a different human because of my experiences with people who are not like me. Hope is rekindled in me through each of these experiences— they help me see the fullness of God. Without each piece and each person, the "quilt" is not complete. As we take bold steps in hope for transformation, joining our stories with the likes of John Wesley and other faithful people, we know that one day Hope will be complete.

Hope: An Antidote for Despair

When I first met "Tony," I was so hopeful that with a good friend and advocate, the right meds, counseling, housing, and healthcare, he would get better. I had been warned that no one had been able to get through to this guy, but I held out hope that I could make a difference. After some time though, hope began to fade—at least in the form that it initially took. Nothing seemed to bring him out of the severe mental health issues that caused him repeated self-destruction. When you do everything you humanly know you can do and destruction continues, what then? When presence is all you can give and nothing else, despair can set in. Despair . . . that is the antithesis of hope.

From the experiences with friends like "Tony" or communal issues like the criminalization of the poor and chronic homelessness, I spend my time moving between despair and hope. It's a cycle that all of us as human beings experience. After the flood of 2010 in Nashville, those with power and resources couldn't seem to get it together to pull more than some hotel rooms together for a week or two. Nashville's most vulnerable residents finding permanent housing solutions wasn't a priority. Charity and mercy were present, but where was the justice?

Can you imagine the collective yearning of an entire nation praying for a savior to rescue them from the pain of oppression?

Maybe Mary and Joseph felt like they were walking through a valley at times. Mary was carrying *the Hope* and those around her didn't even provide a comfortable place for her to rest on the journey. "How long O Lord?" has been our perpetual cry. This is our faith history. People were looking for something beyond everyday hope: the Hope that would "[fill] the hungry with good things" (Luke 1:53a NRSV); the Hope that would bring empathy (Luke 1:52) as people walk a mile in one another's shoes; the Hope that fulfills a lasting promise (Luke 1:54-55). I have to believe that Mary and Joseph moved frequently between despair and hope as they navigated the reality of her pregnancy and all that it would mean for them and for all God's people.

We still cry out today. We move between despair and hope again and again, especially if we are living in intentional community with those who suffer. We want things to permanently be alright and they just aren't going to be. Not in this life.

Ezekiel's vision of a valley of dry bones (Ezekiel 37) both described and inspired our experience during the flood of 2010. Kind of ironic, isn't it, to experience the presence of dry bones during a flood? But that vision—of life and breath returning in the midst of defeat and death—captured for us what it felt like to live with hope in the aftermath of the flood and in the face of indifference from many within our city. After the flood, I made a mobile out of bones I collected from our family farm. It's kinda gross, I know. But the clacking of the bones every time the wind blows through them reminds me of the Holy Spirit breathing life into those dry bones in Ezekiel. This was the sound we imagined when church communities began responding to our cry for temporary housing in churches after the flood. Hope was arising as the Holy Spirit breathed life into these faith communities who offered gymnasiums and fellowship halls as the city told everyone they must leave the temporary shelter given at the height of the crisis.

In the 1990s, just about every preacher I knew told a story about a little girl who kept begging her parents to stay with her as she went to sleep. The mom said, "Go back to bed. God is with you." After getting this answer one too many times, the little girl responded, "But I want somebody with skin on!"

Despair happens when skin doesn't show up.

Hope is ready to breathe life into dry bones, saying, "I am breathing life into you! You go and be the skin!" We have to be the skin for one another because all of us experience despair.

Dry bones had to become flesh for that to happen. People who had been unconscious about the suffering of others started coming to life. The flood happened to everybody and instead of our friends being blamed for their homelessness, they became part of a collective "we." It's sad that it didn't last longer. We still move in and out of despair and hope.

Perspective really helps when we experience despair. It helped that I had done an internship at the General Board of Church and Society during seminary. I saw how much The United Methodist Church is doing throughout the world with an entire agency dedicated to the work of justice. Because I was in DC I got to hear wisdom firsthand from the Dalai Lama and Archbishop Desmond Tutu—people who had experienced things far more horrific than anything I had ever experienced and here they were on the other side of it talking to *me*. So, if you're going through a struggle right now, just remember you are not alone.

An Altogether Hope

What if we brought all the pieces of your life and mine and sewed them together as a quilt? Would we see common threads of hope woven throughout? Would your pieces teach me something new about God? By seeing these common threads would we experience an altogether hope . . . one for all of Creation?

Over two thousand years ago, Hope showed up in a baby, the best symbol of hope there is! Hope was laid in a manger—literally a feeding trough—a sign that generations could feed on this Hope to keep going. God showed up in the last place anybody would choose to give birth, showing us that no place on earth is beyond Hope's reach.

The people I meet on the streets mirror how God showed up then and keeps showing up now. We need to be open to those we meet along the way who show what hope looks like in different places. Each of us carries a piece that is meant to be shared.

Sometimes those we meet—whether in person or not—remind us of what hope looks like when it's inclusive of everyone. This kind of hope can change unjust systems and the world! Mahatma Gandhi gave hope to people on the margins who thought they were powerless and together they experienced a power greater than any one of them could have manifested alone. Martin Luther King Jr. brought hope to those who had systematically been subjugated for hundreds of years, and they are still liberating us today from a culture that's often hope-defying.

Hope travels. When one person gets it, a string of others catch it. At first it came to me through my nuclear family. Then it was the relationships along the way. Now it is the beloved community of all those I've come to know and love. And as it moved outward, it grew from an almost to an altogether hope— one that envisions the well-being of the whole world.

The foundation of my hope has rested in God and God's people. We get it wrong sometimes, but God doesn't. And that thread that we will see raised when we find an altogether hope? It may just be found once again in the most unexpected place.

First Peter 1:3-5 (NRSV) says "Blessed be the God and Father of our Lord Jesus Christ! By his great mercy he has given us a new birth into a living hope through the resurrection of Jesus Christ from the dead, and into an inheritance that is imperishable, undefiled, and unfading, kept in heaven for you, who are being protected by the power of God through faith for a salvation ready to be revealed in the last time."

God has made a place for you at the table.

Questions for Reflection

1. Think about a situation in your life that has seemed hopeless. In what ways did you make your way through?

2. What strange places are you willing to go for hope to be reborn?

3. In what ways can you embody hope for those who have been marginalized within your friends and family? within your church or social groups? within the world?

Hymn Reflection

"Come, Thou Long-Expected Jesus"
(*The United Methodist Hymnal*, 196)

Jesus is the ultimate hope expressed in the Bible. For John Wesley, being an altogether Christian allows us to experience fully the hope of the glory of God. Charles Wesley's hymn "Come, Thou Long-Expected Jesus" powerfully expresses the eternal nature of this hope found in the person of Jesus.

This hymn appears as the tenth of eighteen hymns in Charles's collection *Hymns for the Nativity of our Lord* of 1744. In 1745, the collection was reprinted in Philadelphia by Robert Williams and was one of the first books meant for a continuing group of Methodists in America (*Companion to The United Methodist Hymnal*, p. 91). The fact that the strongly Advent text is in a Christmas collection points to a paradox that is evident in our observation of Advent: we celebrate the "already" nature of Jesus' redemptive actions, but also acknowledge the "not quite" of the ultimate fulfillment of those same salvific actions. This hymn expresses this contradiction in Charles's expectedly artful way.

The United Methodist Hymnal prints the hymn in two stanzas of eight lines. The first stanza begins with an exhortation to the divine: "Come, thou long-expected Jesus." The verb "come" implies "you are not here, come to us." The stanza then outlines the ways in which Jesus fulfills three of the traditional Advent themes: "*hope* of all the earth thou art," "let us find our rest in thee (*personal peace*)," "dear desire of every nation (*corporate*

59

peace)," and "*joy* of every longing heart." This stanza is a strong affirmation that Jesus is the fulfillment of all of the hopes of the world expressed in the Hebrew prophets.

Whereas the first stanza begins with the understanding that Jesus is to come, the second stanza switches tone immediately and uses the past participle of the words *to bear*—born. Here is the paradox: how do we hope for what is not yet while knowing that it has already been?

For Charles, the answer becomes clearer as the second stanza continues. Jesus *was* born as a child and a King to deliver us and reign over God's gracious kingdom *forever*. His birth is both a past and present reality and a promise of future abundant life. Jesus and Jesus only rules in our hearts, and then in the ultimate triumph over the grave, raises us to his glorious throne. This is an ultimate expression of hope.

And if it seems as if the Advent theme of love is missing from this hymn, we should recall John Wesley's emphasis on love as the hallmark of what it means to be an altogether Christian. John asks, "Is the love of God shed abroad in your heart? Can you cry out 'My God and my All!'" Love is the background from which all else radiates, including the hope we have in Jesus' birth.

Jesus, come, be born in our lives again and again, that we may embody the very nature and name of love so that we can be a hope to all the world.

CHAPTER 3

AN ALTOGETHER ℒOVE

APRIL CASPERSON

"And, First, without love nothing can so profit
us as to make our lives happy."
　　　　　　　　—John Wesley, "On Love"[1]

My closest friend asked me to preside over her wedding. She
and her now-husband each have a background in Christianity
and church, but did not actively practice any faith at the time.
As the three of us planned out the ceremony, we all met in the
middle in terms of topics and language. The service would
honor a diverse community coming to celebrate a marriage, and
it would also be Christian and Trinitarian. When I asked them
what they wanted me to preach on, they asked me to preach on
how love overcomes evil.

I struggled in the weeks before the service because I
wanted to hold fast both to my faith and to my desire to lead a

Christian service that would be gracious, welcoming, and able to be received by persons who did not profess a faith. I wanted the themes of the Christian faith to be heard and welcomed in a group that included people who would be disinterested or even hostile to Christianity.

I typically write out my sermon manuscripts, but I didn't even have a sermon outline for this one. I had no words on the page at all in the hours before the service. I was worried that my barely admitted, irrational hopes about love would be just a little too much for this group.

I am not someone who usually wings it, and to have silence from the Spirit as I was writing the liturgy was unsettling, to say the least. The day arrived, and the ceremony began. We prayed, we blessed the gathering, we read poetry and Scripture, and then I found myself speaking on the topic of love.

I told the gathered community about how St. Augustine struggled to reconcile the truth that God created all things with the presence of evil in the world. Did God create evil? Or did God not create everything after all? Eventually, I told them, Augustine came to the realization that since evil is not created by God, evil is somehow a "no thing." This was a very simplified explanation of a complex philosophical idea. And yet, I said that when we are able to acknowledge that evil, while it impacts us, is a "no thing," then we are able to conquer it. I then went on to relate the power of love to conquer:

> We all have different understandings of the Divine in this room. But we came together to honor a shared value: love. Goodness is stronger

than evil, and love is stronger than hate. Love is the thing that conquers evil—love cannot be confined, it cannot be destroyed, it cannot be crushed. Love will enter into any space that is considered to be a "no thing." It fills up that space, and it transforms darkness into light.

An altogether love has that kind of power. It's like shining a light into darkness.

Almost Love

Too often, we settle for an "almost love" instead of the real thing. We content ourselves with a pale beam that leaves plenty of shadows rather than a bright illumination that can fill the world. An "almost love" is a love that welcomes only the parts of people that are desirable, or palatable, or easy to handle. In contrast, an "altogether love"—the evil-conquering kind of love—is a love that welcomes the whole self and honors that we are made up of many parts. An altogether love is cross-cultural and countercultural. It can seem irrational to love in this way—or even to *be loved* in this way.

It is dangerous to allow our full selves to be shown to the world, because there is always the fear that if someone really knew us, we would not be lovable. The culture in many online spaces allows and encourages us to show only our best moments publicly: the snapshot from the vacation, the staged photo of the family, a pretty picture of a sunset. Without even realizing it, we end up presenting that to the world as the totality of our human life. Sometimes we push the limits a bit and share a carefully curated picture of a "hard day," a portrait of ourselves with tired eyes or no makeup on, or we share a few vague phrases about a troubling situation. What we present may be honest sharing, but it is still easily digestible. These selected bits and pieces still ensure that we are lovable to those who consume our online personas. Those we encounter online love us, but it is an "almost love" because they encounter an "almost us."

I may be so bold as to say that we even bring these worthy but fragmented slices of ourselves to church. We present them to our fellow Christians as our whole selves, ensuring that we are still worthy of their love on Sunday mornings; that we still belong; that we still "fit" into the community of faith. Many of my colleagues who pastor churches share that people thinking about coming to a church for the first time usually ask, "What do people wear there?" as one of their first questions. Even when we hunger for Christian community, we worry about whether our full selves will be welcomed in the church.

It is almost as though it is easier for us to talk about love and how we want to be loved by staying in the careful realm of "almost love"—presenting piecemeal selves to the world that are not too offensive, not too much, nice and pleasant in an easily consumable way. Unable or unwilling to risk being loved altogether, we strive for an almost love because we think that's better than nothing. Perhaps we don't really believe in the truth that instead of being confined and oppressed into an almost, we can step into an altogether version of ourselves as Christians and as the church. Perhaps we don't believe the truth that love, real love, is waiting for us.

John Wesley and an Almost Love

I appreciate John Wesley because he truly grappled with what it meant to be an ethical, moral, good person. He came to see love as the key to it all. Wesley spent years trying to explain how God's love changes our lives even as we are flawed human beings. As he wrestled with these challenging topics, he grounded his reflections in the reality that we as humans are impacted by a force outside of ourselves: the grace and love of God.

It can be problematic to name Christianity as the pinnacle of morality. Wesley talked about "heathen honesty." The language is dated and even offensive when we read it today, but this vocabulary was Wesley's way to remind his readers that morality was not only owned by Christians. In the same way, in his sermon "The Almost Christian" he laid the groundwork for how some people who are not Christian can and do live out moral, ethical, and loving lives.

> They expected whatever assistance any one could give another, without prejudice to himself. And this they extended not only to those little offices of humanity which are performed without any expense or labour, but likewise to the feeding the hungry, if they had food to spare; the clothing the naked with their own superfluous raiment; and, in general, the giving, to any that needed, such things as they needed not themselves.[2]

In other words, the non-Christian can be ethical, moral, and even loving in his or her actions. Then Wesley goes on to explain how even a superficial Christian can carry out a loving lifestyle. This "almost Christian" is a loving person, caring for creation, exerting self-control, and even engaging in the practice of religion:

> To this, if we add the constant use of family prayer by those who are masters of families, and the setting times apart for private addresses to God, with a daily seriousness of behaviour; he who uniformly practises this outward religion, has the form of godliness.[3]

What is the "almost" according to John Wesley? The almost Christian, the woman or man living in almost love—this person is not bad or evil, but this person does exhibit a lack of depth. The almost Christian is characterized by outward actions, thoughts, and feelings that do not penetrate all the way to the heart.

This understanding of surface-level feeling and action is so relevant today. How many of us find ourselves doing the right things or "performing morality" without diving into a deeper reason for why we do what we do?

Today we run into this very Wesleyan understanding of almost love when it comes to what it means to be a church and a community of faith. Even the most committed Christian may find herself or himself somewhat dismayed at a Sunday morning worship experience. We all want to "feel good" when we come to church—to hear an uplifting message, sing and hear music that speaks to us, and to be reminded of God's active role in our lives. But we also long for more than a superficial experience of temporary happiness. We long for the truth of the wonder, mystery, hope, and love of God in our lives.

Have you ever reluctantly confessed to a friend that going to church feels good, but sometimes the experience feels like it misses the mark? Or have you had someone tell you kindly but firmly that they believe in God and Jesus but don't care much for religion because it doesn't talk as much about love as they would hope? Have you ever heard a sermon that, upon reflection, only included instructions on "being a good person" and didn't include any substantive insights about how God is working in our lives?

Churches often do good in the world, and churches are for many people simply another one of the organizations they join in order to do good in the world. It can be dangerous when, as Frank Thomas has said, churches "do good things just because we think they are good ideas."[4] Doing good in the world—by any motivation—is not evil or malicious. But good and helpful are not the same thing. "Good" can be subjective. Doing good because something is a good idea is a great Wesleyan example of an "almost love."

Wesley makes the case that someone can be good, kind, moral, and even love rightly without having depth—but the person is then just a surface-level person of faith. It is almost as if Wesley would say that someone who demonstrates love through a misplaced motivation—such as for profit, admiration, or influence—isn't necessarily evil. They are just superficial— exhibiting a life of "almost love."

In contrast to an almost love, an altogether love runs deep, all the way to our heart. Good deeds come from an altogether love not out of obligation or because they are a good idea, but because they are the natural expression of love. In other words, they are love in action. And as the Advent season and Scriptures remind us, this kind of love is risky, requiring hope and even seeming at times to be irrational.

Advent: The Now and the Not Yet

Advent is an affirmation of the now and the not yet. I love Advent precisely because we don't have the whole story in front of us, and in that there is a sense of hopefulness—a sense of the world pointing in a specific direction, toward an unexpected thing that is deeply irrational. How in the world could a baby be something so powerful that it has transformed all of creation?

I served on staff at Methodist Theological School in Ohio, a United Methodist seminary, for over ten years, and it was a wonderful season. I am so thankful for the experiences on that campus. Part of what I loved at the school was being around people who were just simply *hopeful*—they were living in the now and the not yet. These people were taking a leap into a commitment to work on a degree that would take three to four years. They were committing to a vocation where they didn't know where they would serve, or what that would look like exactly, or how that would sound, or even who they would be in that next season. As an academic and learning community, we were consistently hopeful about the future and hopeful about what could come out of these students, the scholarship, the administration. It was a place where hope lives—a perpetual Advent season, if you will.

For part of my time at the school, my role was to interact with potential and current students to talk about goals, academic pathways, and hopes for lay and ordained ministry in a variety of denominational traditions. I look back at those conversations and have vivid memories of sitting across from one another at a table, or in the dining hall, or talking to one another on the phone, sharing and visioning what could be and what it would take to get there. I even have visual memories of certain email conversations where we collaborated to bring forth a new vision of vocation and hope. In hindsight, those personal conversations feel like Advent moments—moments where we saw abundant possibilities for the future without having the whole story in front of us.

So many of those conversations had a layer of irrationality to them, I must confess. Considering academic study in the fields of divinity, counseling, theology, and ethics is a worthy endeavor. It is also decidedly *not* a guaranteed pathway to financial stability, especially when compared to many other vocational fields. In the same way, considering a life of ministry as a vocation, either as a clergyperson or a thoughtfully committed layperson, is compelling but not always rational. The work is challenging, the values are countercultural, the unknown factors are substantial, and faithful service requires the entire self. It is so much like Advent.

Advent is about willingly engaging in generative and regenerative work. Advent is a fresh start and a season of revisioning what could happen. And Advent is a willingness to look into the future and be willing to embrace the irrational as the way of love. In the Advent narrative, God uses normal people in very unexpected, irrational ways.

Advent, Love, and Mary's Pause

In Luke's Gospel, the account of Mary's pregnancy focuses on Mary's perspective and that of her cousin Elizabeth. Joseph is barely mentioned, and we have no information about what he was thinking or pondering throughout the story. It is as though God selected women to articulate what it means when God enters the world in irrational and unexpected ways.

Luke's story of the angel's appearance to Mary contains many layers. Especially striking is Mary's response, her deliberate consent to bearing the Christ Child. Oftentimes when we consider Advent (whether preaching it, worshiping in Advent, or participating in our community Advent traditions) we default to a simplistic celebration of a linear story: an angel appeared to Mary, Mary became pregnant with the Christ Child, and then the Christ saves the world. But if we take our time and really dig in, we can illuminate so much more about the Advent story and the unexpected ways in which God transforms the almost into an altogether.

In the first chapter of Luke, we find a teenager who is visited by an angel in the middle of the night. In the moment when the angel first speaks to Mary and tells her that she is going to bear the Christ Child, Mary doesn't say yes, and she doesn't say no. She stops the angel's proclamation and whatever is going to come next, and she asks a question. That's a remarkable response. Mary has the boldness to make the angel stop what he is saying so that she can ask a question.

> Mary said to the angel, "How can this be, since I am a virgin?" The angel said to her, "The Holy Spirit will come upon you, and the power of the Most High will overshadow you; therefore the child to be born will be holy; he will be called Son of God. And now, your relative Elizabeth in her old age has also conceived a son; and this is the sixth month for her who was said to be barren. For nothing will be impossible with God. Then Mary said, "Here am I, the servant of the Lord; let it be with me according to your word." Then the angel departed from her. (Luke 1:34-38 NRSV)

It is so very important to understand that Mary asked the angel to slow down—especially since Zechariah had been chastised for questioning an angel in a similar situation only a few verses earlier (Luke 1:20). In the middle of an angelic proclamation, Mary asked for more details. The angel gave them to her, and then the angel waited for her to respond. Then and only then did Mary say yes. Mary's question highlights the uncertainty in her present and future. She wants a little more information before stepping out into the unknown. And that yes, that willingness to take on the unknown, that welcome to be used by God? It was an act of altogether love.

Pregnancy and childbirth are taxing and dangerous. That's true even today, even for those of us who have access to modern medicine. Despite our privilege, pregnancy, childbirth, and the postpartum experience are still profoundly dangerous, both mentally and physically. For Mary, in her time, place, and situation, the stakes were breathtakingly high. So it is important to note that the angel did not promise her survival. She was told that her name would be remembered, but not reassured that she would live through her experience. Mary had to know of many of the potential consequences of saying yes to God with whole self and taking an unknown step into love. And yet she chose love.

Have you had experiences in your life where you stood at the beginning of a new season and said yes to love without knowing how it would all turn out? When we open ourselves to wonder and love, we are reminded that we are not the center of the universe. If our ability to be loved was rooted in our flawed selves, there is no way that we would ever be worthy of love. But God gently meets us in our imperfections, God pauses for us to ask questions, and then God welcomes us with open arms into an altogether love.

Wesley and the Private Life

One important thread in Wesley's understanding of love is based in privacy and an intimate, nonpublic relationship between God and the Christian. Wesley's faith progression was rooted in personal transformation and a continual reaching toward holiness. His sermons and letters, while oftentimes intended for a wider audience, reflect his own faith development and growing understanding of God's love for us. In the same way, the Advent narrative lays out how normal humans were visited by God, how they were changed by that experience, and then how they ran out into the world to proclaim an altogether love. Immediately after Gabriel visited Mary, the young woman went "with haste" (1:39 NRSV) to visit her cousin Elizabeth. They processed the news together, celebrating and allowing God's love to work in them privately before Mary's pregnancy would become broadly known.

In many situations, privacy invites true honesty. Wesley sought for the Christian to be honest, authentic, and loving. Advent invites us to enter into a season of reflection where we become honest with ourselves and consider what it means to bring our whole selves to God. What does it mean when we encounter the Advent narrative that sheds light on the imperfections of the human actors in the story? God's love encounters flawed human beings and moves them from imperfection—an almost Christian—to people who are fully used, known, and surrounded with an altogether love.

Earlier I shared about some of my experiences working with students pursuing careers in ministry as laity and clergy. Many of those conversations were private and personal. Oftentimes my team and I would hear students say, "I've never shared this with anyone before, but this is what would make me truly joyful. Doing this work is what I love."

I share that these conversations were private not because they were secret or secretive, but because they were honest and intimate forms of sharing. For Wesley, the Christian life steeped in love had some outward signs, but the hallmark of the love of a

Christian was that faithfulness was practiced in private—much like Mary's conversation with the angel and her subsequent decision to accept love and the unknown.

I am currently serving with my annual conference in diversity and inclusion. My service includes helping equip our clergy, laity, local churches, and regional structures to better work across differences. Sometimes our conversations begin with race. Other times we begin conversations around income, gender, age, or politics. We have found there to be great impact when leadership teams, clergy communities, and committees engage in this work together. But a lot of the transformation takes place in private—when participants are reading and reflecting on their own, or when they are willing to have deep, honest, private one-on-one conversations with a colleague or a coach.

It can be a very scary thing to talk to someone who is different from you and to discuss race, politics, theology, or other forms of diversity. There is the potential for great growth, learning, and change when groups get together to talk about these topics. I have observed deep change when people have honest, one-on-one conversations where they have the safety and opportunity to share their full experiences with one another. It takes time to build relationships and trust another person. But when we take the time to be in genuine relationship, we eventually can stop presenting an "almost self" and share our "altogether self." Privacy and intimacy allow us to move from an almost to an altogether love.

Being Fully Known and Loved

I wonder how much of our insecurity about trusting that God fully loves us is because we live so much of our lives in public. In other words, we probably wonder if God really can love us fully as we are. The world is a dangerous place when we dare to reveal (or are unable to hide) our imperfections. Or perhaps we worry that we are not "good enough" for God to use us for change in the world just as we are. And yet, the gift of a private relationship between God and each of us is one of the ways in which God reminds us that we are fully loved, and that God can use us for good just as we are.

Mary's Magnificat in Luke 1:46-55 is a continuation of the celebration of God's love and favor. It is a flowing, emotional, prophetic poem that belongs to her and her alone. Her expression of altogether love is written in Luke's Gospel in a form that is intended to be shared with the world, but her poetry has shades of personal experience and even an inner monologue. It is an expression of love that was created in privacy, intended to reflect her inner thoughts and then to be shared with the world.

Sometimes God creates spaces where we have privacy, and we can sit in those private spaces and realize that even though love is always surrounding us, sometimes God will show kindness to us and give us a holy space to reflect and ponder. It is in these holy, private connections between us and God that we can decide to say yes to love—to move from an almost love, a love held at arm's length, to an altogether love, a love that we fully embrace, even as God has been there all along.

Love Shows Up

For Wesley, love is a part and parcel of both the human experience and God's care for us. Faith is a mindset and a response to the gift of unmerited grace we have received from God, but faith is also intimately connected to action. The act of loving—love of God, love of self, love of neighbor, love of the world—is an engaged and deliberate choice in a person's life.

Wesley wraps up his understanding of love within thoughtful, God-inspired, and directed action—loving one's neighbor, taking risks into an unknown future, and orienting the mind toward an ultimate hope. Our Advent story, centered around the risk-taking love that Mary chose, reminds us that it is dangerous to love fully, but that we are offered the opportunity to love over and over again, oftentimes in unexpected places.

Wesley viewed faith formation through the experience of grace as a continual, lifelong process, like a rich tapestry of personal and community stories where love just keeps showing up. One of the joys of a biblical narrative is that we as readers are invited to imagine what happens in between stories. How often did Mary have the opportunity to fall in love with her son over and over again as he moved from childhood to adulthood? How many times did she choose to continue to love him, to keep her presence with him even as he journeyed toward the cross? Wesley reminds us that he moved through his faith and continually fell in love with God, the church, and the community of faith throughout his life.

In the Advent narrative, God shows up as an act of altogether love. But the humans in the stories also showed up in their own ways, moving from an almost love to an altogether, active love that proclaimed salvation to the world. Mary said yes to an unknown future; Elizabeth sheltered Mary in the face of the unknown. In our faith, God shows up as an act of love, and our response to God's altogether love is to show up and go out into the world with the good news of Christ.

Advent and the Worship Experience

Advent brings us a multitude of opportunities to move from the almost to the altogether. The clichés about the busyness of the Christmas season, the admonishments around consumerism, and the pressure to have a moral, ethical, yet photo-worthy Christmas are loud and distracting. These cultural narratives also set us up to think that we can create, manufacture, and share an "almost-perfect Christmas"—as though we can possess or own a holiday and a moment in the Christian year.

The Advent narrative—women saying yes to love and to the unknown, shepherds saying yes to spreading an irrational, hopeful message, angels who spread the news of a king who intends not to possess and oppress, but to love—this narrative moves us from an almost love to an altogether love. The typical cultural view of the weeks leading up to Christmas urges us to own, to consume, to create, to control. The consumerism and performance culture of our time whispers to us, "If you do these things, then you will own and win Christmas." So in response, the church calls us to move into an Advent experience of altogether love, because the opposite of possession and control is love.

Rev. Dr. Frank A. Thomas reminds us that the gospel is the "language of mystery and hope. That's what preaching is."[5] Our call in the Advent season is to help ourselves and one another move from an almost love (a desire to control, shape, and possess a Christmas experience) into an altogether love (a reflection and experience of the mystery, danger, and abundant, unexpected life that comes to us in Christ).

It is so easy to experience Advent worship as a simplistic performance of a familiar story. Sometimes we come to church in Advent or on Christmas and our motivation is to consume and experience a fantastic, memorable worship experience. When we slide into these habits, it is helpful to remember that the reason we worship is to be a part of a story that cannot be found anywhere else. The world promises an almost love. But the Advent story is a reckless narrative—a narrative that places ordinary, unexpected, simple, invisible people at the forefront, placing them smack-dab in the middle of God's great acts in the world. The Advent story is a story of choosing an altogether love that welcomes the whole self and leads into the unknown.

If Communion is a part of your Advent worship experiences, be sure that when you go up to the Communion table you remember that God loves us just as we are, and that all are welcome at the Communion table. This radical truth is in direct contrast with our surrounding culture that often demands perfection before people share their whole selves in public. You may have even had some painful previous church and faith experiences in another religious community. Advent is a fantastic time to come to the table with fresh eyes and a fresh heart—because the altogether love of Advent welcomes you to Communion just as you are.

In the Advent season, your call is to help yourself, your family, and your church community move from a secular almost love—be a good person, be good people together, do good together at Christmastime—to an altogether love. God speaks from a place of altogether love. God says, "Come and be altogether loved. Come and hear My story that asked normal people into an altogether love, where all parts of you are used and loved and valued. There is a risk in bringing your whole self to Me, but the reward is immeasurable." Bring your entire self to worship—your childhood memories of Christmas, the relationships that bring either tension or love, or both, in the Christmas season, and your hope for a transformation through Christ.

An Irrational Act

It can be dangerous and irrational to fully embrace love. The experience and sometimes even the concept of radical, unconditional, unmerited love is foreign to our world, and oftentimes when we try to share love, we present love as being attached to *us* somehow—to our achievements, to connection to a particular church or kind of church, or to conformity. And yet, John Wesley reminds us of the reckless, unmerited love of God that pulls us into relationship with Jesus Christ, oftentimes and even before we are aware of it.

The church does not own love. Humanity does not own love. Love is too big, too inclusive, too rule-breaking, too reckless to be confined. When we try to define love by simply human terms, we may do good things in the world but we are still stuck in an almost love. The funny thing is that we can't own or conquer love. Every time we try to confine where love belongs or where love "should" show up, it will pop up in the most unexpected place.

The world was in an almost state when God began showing up and pulling flawed, ordinary human beings into the Advent story. God showed up in the middle of the night in the room of a teenage girl, in the middle of a field to a bunch of shepherds, and in the arms of Elizabeth as she protected her cousin in the face of the unknown. God's presence in the lives of ordinary people transformed them from the almost to the altogether.

Advent reminds us that love shows up in the most unexpected places, transforming flawed, imperfect people into people redeemed by love. God compels us to move from an almost love (the love that we think is based upon who we are and what we do) into an altogether love (a love that grows to fill all spaces, bringing light wherever there is darkness).

Questions for Reflection

1. How are you being asked to fall in love with God again and again in this season of your life?

2. How do you present an "almost self" to the world? What would change if you presented an "altogether self" to the world? to your church community? to God?

3. In an Advent worship experience, what would help you feel fully embraced by God's altogether love?

4. What barriers in your faith journey have you encountered that seem to keep you at arm's length from fully embracing God's love?

Hymn Reflection

"Love Divine, All Loves Excelling"
(*The United Methodist Hymnal*, 384)

"Love divine, all loves excelling, joy of heaven, to earth come down. . . . Jesus, thou art all compassion, pure, unbounded love thou art." There can be no mistaking, Charles Wesley believes that Jesus is an altogether love. The text of this hymn ascribes the powers of an altogether love to each part of the Trinity and then provides a fitting prayer for our place in that divine, all-excelling, altogether love of God.

The hymn first appeared in Strahan's "Hymns for Those that Seek and Those that Have Redemption in the Blood of Jesus Christ," of 1747. It is the ninth of the collection's fifty-two hymns, most of which can be traced to Charles. As the title of the collection suggests, the hymns give voice to people in various stages of the spiritual journey; in a sense, each hymn echoes the idea of becoming an altogether Christian.

The first verse begins with a fitting plea for Advent: Jesus, come to earth. The writer is saying, make in us a humble dwelling, much like the humble manger in which Jesus was placed. Charles goes on to list two names for Jesus: "all compassion" and "pure, unbounded love." The verse ends with another plea, that Jesus would enter every unsteady heart and bring his salvation.

The second verse addresses the Holy Spirit. Again, the verse starts with a plea—this time for the Spirit to breathe into every troubled breast. Quickly the text presents the concept of the second rest—that is, that all have an inheritance and share in Christ's Second Coming. The third line contains a central theological concept in John Wesley's theology, Christian Perfection. Though central to Wesleyan theology, its appearance in this hymn proved troubling. The original line is "take away our power of sinning." Such a plea violates the idea of free will, and sets up an unreal expectation of Christian perfection. For these reasons, the verse has been left out of many hymnals since its first publication. *The United Methodist Hymnal* uses an altered version of the text that is more palatable: "Take away our bent to sinning." The verse ends with a realization that God is the beginning and ending and has the power to set us free.

The Almighty Godhead is the focus in the third verse. Pleas for godly life and God's ever presence in our lives give way to our response. We will bless and serve you as the angels, pray and praise without ending, and glory in God's perfect love. This approaches the altogether love that John Wesley means when he writes, "He that thus loves the Lord his God, his spirit continually 'rejoiceth in God his Saviour.'"[6]

The final verse gives a glimpse of the glorious conclusion of God's love that has turned our hearts to him. We are the new creation that sees the great and perfect salvation, as we take our place in heaven and get lost altogether "in wonder, love, and praise."

CHAPTER 4

AN ALTOGETHER *JOY*

MATT RAWLE

"Joy: that durable, inexhaustible, essential, inadequate word."[1]

Christmas is so close. The anticipation is palpable, but what is it that we are anticipating? Are we filled with an almost insatiable and expectant joy to welcome Christ in the world? Maybe we are embarrassingly excited about what we might find under the tree? We know intuitively that there is a real difference between joy at Christ's coming—what we experience when we sing "Joy to the World" with a heart of faith—and the happiness we feel when our Christmas list is fulfilled after all the presents have been opened. But what exactly is the difference?

As we make our final movement around the Advent wreath, we light the candle of joy last at the church I serve. Other congregations often light the joy candle on the third Sunday of Advent, but I find celebrating joy on the fourth Sunday to be a powerful witness to the meaning of Christ's coming. Our anticipation rests and finds its culmination in joy, in the steadfast assurance that God is with us. This feeling sometimes occurs alongside happiness and frivolity. Other times joy somehow blooms in the midst of difficulty and despair. Joy is profound because it supersedes the fleeting offerings of happiness and sadness. An "Almost joy," although powerful, never remains. But an "Altogether joy" defies category and is nearly inexplicable.

So, how do we move from an almost joy to an altogether joy? I'm sad to say that if you are looking to experience joy through words on a page, you are looking in the wrong place (says the guy writing about joy). Joy cannot be manufactured, sought, or studied. In the same way that it is impossible to tickle yourself, joy is not something you can achieve. An altogether joy is a gift. This steadfast assurance that God is with us is experienced as the unexpected fulfillment of anticipation. What better time to ponder it than in the final week of Advent, just before we welcome Christ as God with us.

A Fleeting, Almost Joy

There is little joy in the Gospel of Mark. At least, the word *joy* is found only once (Mark 4:16) and in a context not immediately relevant for our Advent waiting. When thinking about joy as part of our Advent journey, there's little from Mark's Gospel that can help guide our meditation. Mark is fast-paced and action-packed, containing only information that seems absolutely necessary to reveal the mystery of Christ as the Messiah.

Mark's Gospel is so hurried that Jesus appears almost out of nowhere with no mention of angels, shepherds, wise men, the manger, Bethlehem, or even Joseph. It seems that Mark wanted to jump right into the action of Jesus' story without pausing to rejoice in its beginning.

If I'm honest, maybe I'm more like Mark during Advent than I care to admit. I always light the candle of joy on the last Sunday of Advent with a bit of regret. Like Mark, I find myself too busy to have left room for joy. When I light the last Advent candle I feel a sense of dread, recognizing that no matter how the calendar falls, there's no more than a week left before Christmas Eve. My guilt usually isn't about lack of time to finalize family gatherings, gifts, or travel plans because that is precisely what I've been doing for four weeks. My dread is that the season is almost over, and I've left little room for what the candles actually represent.

This is why Luke appropriately holds our attention more the closer we move toward Christmas. Luke's Gospel is saturated with joy. Luke takes the time to reveal that joy is present even before Jesus is born. "You will have joy and gladness" is the first promise offered in the Gospel when Zechariah discovers his wife, Elizabeth, who was thought to be barren, will have a child (Luke 1:14 NRSV). But this great promise of joy is met with disbelief, causing Zechariah to become mute and unable to speak, "until the day these things occur" (Luke 1:20 NRSV). At first it seems that Zechariah's inability to speak is a punishment or a curse, but maybe we could all do with more silence leading up to Christmas Eve. Slowing down to leave room for joy often takes more listening than speaking. Perhaps Zechariah's silence was a gift rather than a curse, an opportunity given by the angel for Zechariah to experience joy as he looked forward to his son's birth.

One of the most meaningful worship experiences we have in our congregation is a "Longest Night" service. In the last days leading up to Christmas, we gather in the sanctuary for a moment of silence and communion. A single guitar offers songs that speak honestly to the pain and sorrow many feel during a season in which most are occupied with happiness and merriment. The extended silence in the service was particularly moving for a woman in our church one year. She shared that the silence she experienced was the first time in recent memory that no one was asking her to be something she isn't. She said that through the parties, preparations, and family gatherings she felt that she needed to "put on a happy face" so she wouldn't ruin Christmas for anyone. She had lost a child years ago during the holiday season, and she felt the pain always needed to be hidden. In a very real sense, the silence she experienced in the darkened sanctuary gave her permission to put down the mask she felt she needed to wear. It was a beautiful and poignant moment of honesty she desperately needed. Silence was a gift to her, and I daresay that despite her pain, joy came to her in the honesty silence afforded. In a similar way, I wonder if Zechariah's silence created space for him to experience joy. Zechariah had doubted that the joy the angel announced would be possible, so the angel gave a second announcement that Zechariah would remain silent until his joy was fulfilled. Although I can't conceive how you might place this under a tree, silence is sometimes the very gift we need for joy to be experienced.

Joy is often thought to be a happy feeling, but this is not altogether correct. At least, Luke's Gospel offers a curious context for joy. Not long after the angel Gabriel makes another visit, this time to Mary, she travels to visit Elizabeth who is pregnant with John. John in Elizabeth's womb "leaped for joy," when Mary and Elizabeth met (Luke 1:44 NRSV). Initially, this seems like an exuberance or gladness, but if we keep reading Luke's Gospel we will discover that the only other time we find the phrase "leap for joy" is when Jesus says, "Blessed are you when people hate you . . . leap for joy, for surely your reward is great in heaven" (Luke 6:22-23 NRSV). It seems that John's leaping foreshadows his own rejection at the hands of King Herod. In Luke's Gospel, joy comes after silence, and it is experienced in the midst of persecution. This is a far cry from what we typically recognize as joy during the Advent and Christmas season. Joy certainly can be happy and cheerful, but this "almost joy" misses the fullness of what Scripture seems to say about the joy we feel as followers of Christ.

Wesley, Joy, and Salvation

Once I've made it to the fourth week of Advent I begin to get very excited about Christmas Eve worship. One of my favorite experiences of the entire year is singing "Silent Night" by candlelight. It may sound selfish, but it is very reassuring that no matter how good or bad a Christmas Eve sermon may be, "Silent Night" is there to bring us home with a sense of beauty, peace, and holiness. Singing "Silent Night" by candlelight is an almost universal way to end a Christmas Eve service. No matter the denomination, time of service, or number of people packed into a sanctuary, "Silent Night" by candlelight seems to speak beyond our petty (or maybe not so petty) Christian squabbles to offer a beauty that we can all appreciate.

But "Silent Night" isn't the only song to leap over denominational walls. The great Charles Wesley hymn "Hark! the Herald Angels Sing" also seems to be universally accepted across most faith communities, and it is a hymn that beautifully expresses Christian joy. The first verse of the hymn reads:

> Hark! the herald angels sing,
> "Glory to the newborn King;
> peace on earth, and mercy mild,
> God and sinners reconciled!"
>
> Joyful, all ye nations rise,
> join the triumph of the skies;
> with th'angelic host proclaim,
> "Christ is born in Bethlehem!"

The last line of the first stanza sets the tone for how John and Charles Wesley understood the nature of joy: "God and sinners reconciled." For Wesley, salvation and joy go hand in hand. There is no joy for those who feel there is no forgiveness. There is no joy for those who have no assurance of salvation. Without joy there is little for which to give thanks. Joy comes from knowing that God is near and salvation is offered to all.

A hymn about salvation being offered to all may be why "Hark" has such a wide acceptance across so many traditions. God and *sinners* are reconciled, not just God and those who make all of the Advent worship opportunities. Joyful, *all ye nations* rise, not just those who share our political beliefs. All people, not just the strongest or most successful, are invited to proclaim Christ's birth. John Wesley wrote, "Speak from my mouth a sacred song. . . . Mercy I sing, transporting sound, / The joy of earth and heaven! / Mercy by every sinner found, / Who takes what GOD hath given. . . . He calls as many souls as breathe, / And all may hear the call. . . . Be justified by faith alone, / And freely saved by grace."[2] Especially during this hectic time of the year, we need to remember that we are justified by faith and freely saved by grace—and that this is altogether joy.

An almost joy is an emotion we often feel during the holiday season because of the numerous good works we are encouraged to offer. More to the point, when we aren't feeling particularly joyful we often find ourselves jumping into a new small group, giving extra to the offering, and volunteering at the local elementary school in order to make us feel good about our Advent preparations. Don't get me wrong; surrounding ourselves with the habits of study, stewardship, and service are good things. But these things alone can only produce an almost joy. The seemingly joyful feeling is often short-lived, and soon we find ourselves overfilling our schedule in order to capture something that these activities simply cannot provide.

When I was a student in middle school, I remember taking lots of time to make my projects look good—making sure the font was attractive, the colored paper on the trifold was pleasing, and the slideshow transitions were perfect. Of course, all of this was at the expense of the work itself. It's like the local science fair when I was in sixth grade and my sister was in fourth. I studied the effectiveness of different household cleaners, and my sister studied the effect of temperature on an electric current. We both placed first in our class in our school's science fair, which meant we qualified for the district science fair. Now, I am not one to shy away from a competition, especially a competition with my little sister.

So, in preparation for the district level I made sure that my graphics were beautiful, the presentation was well rehearsed, and my smile was as charming as possible. My sister, on the other hand, worked on her data, made sure her experiment was airtight, and her conclusion undeniable. Needless to say, I placed second and my sister placed first. I was humiliated that my little sister got the blue ribbon, while I had to settle for being the first loser. She also won't let me forget it. I would love to say that this was the only time my sister got the better of me, but that is laughably false. Now I can admit that every time she raised the bar, she also raised up everyone else. For this, I am truly thankful.

Focusing on our outward actions is like having the paper and presentation beautiful, but lacking in the scientific results. Or it's like setting the Christmas table with china, a beautiful centerpiece, and fancy cloth napkins and forgetting to cook the meal. It's only an almost joy. In contrast, nothing less than God's mercy is the joy of earth and heaven. God's mercy is given to "every sinner found" not just those who have joined the newest small group or tithed or volunteered their time at the local food pantry. Altogether joy comes from an encounter with this mercy, not from the thing we do during the weeks leading up to Christmas. Studying, giving, and serving are fruit of our joy, not the joy itself. Fruit not the root, as I often say.

I love lighting the candle of joy during the last week of Advent. Joy is the culmination of our Advent celebration because joy is a gift. Hope is a future destination for which we dream and work. Peace is a daily discipline to put down the sword in whatever form it is known. Love requires a selflessness in order to be shared. Joy is different from the other candles we light during the season because joy cannot be achieved. Joy simply is a gift. Receiving joy often means we have to get out of the way and allow the Holy Spirit to move. An almost joy is something we can produce. Through presents under the tree, gathering together around the dinner table, and singing the Christmas hymns and songs we love, we can create an environment where we see a glimmer of joy. Yet often, hours after the presents have been opened, family has returned home, and our playlist has changed to New Year's, we feel that something's missing, which means that the joy we felt was not complete. An altogether joy can only be received by God's grace. It remains even when the Christmas tree has been hauled to the curb. It stays with us even when familiar faces are no longer present. Joy "comes in the morning," even when our eyes are used to the dark. As Paul puts it, joy is "the peace of God, which surpasses all understanding" (Philippians 4:7 NRSV). In the last week of Advent, just before we travel to the manger, our souls are ready to receive this precious gift of joy—the steadfast assurance that God is with us.

Christ in the manger is the manifestation of this joy. Not only is God with us, but God has put on flesh and surprisingly entered the world as a baby. "God is with us" is no longer a theological treatise, philosophical framework, or helpful metaphor. Joy now has hands that will be outstretched to bless, comfort, and welcome. These hands also will be outstretched and nailed to the cross because we wanted joy on our own shallow and selfish terms. Joy now has feet that will walk with flawed disciples, feet that will be washed with tears, feet that will traverse into Samaritan land. These feet will also be bound together in an attempt to stop the scandalous work of God's grace, justice, and forgiveness. The presence of God now has a body—a body that will hunger and thirst, heal and feed. This body will be crucified and raised, and by the power of the Holy Spirit, this body will defy time to become those gathered together, from generation to generation, in mutual and shared adoration of God.

This joy is timeless. I am tempted to say that joy lives in the present, but the experience of joy seems almost "other" when talking about a timeline. Chris Wiman said it well: "To define joy as present tense is to keep it fastened to time, and that doesn't feel completely right. It might be truer to say that joy is a flash of eternity that *illuminates* time, but the word 'eternity' does sit a bit lumpishly there on the page."[3]

Have you ever thought about joy as a "flash of eternity"? One afternoon I remember that I was frustrated I had to leave the office early. My wife had to bring one of my daughters to the doctor, so I had to stay at home with our other daughters. My frustration was not with one of my children being sick, but that I was losing time to write my sermon. As a preacher I am always under a hard sermon deadline of 8:30 Sunday morning. There have been times I've been tempted to begin my sermon with "This has been a really long week, so we will be watching a movie in lieu of a sermon," like the blessed days of elementary school when a substitute teacher would roll the TV cart into the room. But (so far) I have not exercised that option. Which means the sermon has to be written.

Once out of the office and at home with my daughters, I sat in the living room trying to mentally map the rest of my sermon. One of my daughters said, "Daddy, do you want to play?" My first reaction was poor. "Not right now, sweetie. Daddy is trying to finish his sermon." When her shoulders slumped and her face pointed to the floor I realized my shortsightedness. "Of course Daddy will play with you," I quickly replied. As I rolled a ball back and forth with my daughter I lost all sense of time. It was like I'd been illuminated by a flash of eternity. In that moment, nothing was more important. It was simple. It was fun. It was joy. Needless to say, the ending of my sermon had written itself.

Funny how joy works that way. We can plan, prepare, primp, and produce, and joy almost mischievously appears when we stop trying to make it appear. This is why joy can only be received, why we celebrate joy at the end of Advent. At this point, preparations must cease. Jesus is going to be born whether you are ready or not. A flash of eternity can only appear when our temporal distractions have been silenced.

Moving to an Altogether Joy

Altogether joy is an encounter with God's mercy. It's a flash of eternity. It is the steadfast assurance that God is with us. This means it can be received even in the midst of pain. I would love to say that joy is always a happy feeling. But our temptation to think that joy is exclusively happy limits our experience only to an almost joy. An altogether joy recognizes that joy can be, maybe most appropriately, experienced in the midst of pain. Joy is not a moment that negates our pain or dismisses it as inconsequential or meaningless. Joy is a steadfast assurance that God is with us always, even if pain is with us too. In a way, joy is a "homesickness for a home you were not aware of having."[4] The Psalms can help us understand these aspects of joy and what it can mean to receive an altogether joy.

One of the most popular Scriptures about joy is Psalm 30 (verses 1-5 NRSV):

> I will extol you, O LORD, for you have drawn me up,
>> and did not let my foes rejoice over me.
> O LORD my God, I cried to you for help,
>> and you have healed me.
> O LORD, you brought up my soul from Sheol,
>> restored me to life from among those gone down
>> to the Pit.
>
> Sing praises to the LORD, O you his faithful ones,
>> and give thanks to his holy name.
> For his anger is but for a moment;
>> his favor is for a lifetime.

Weeping may linger for the night,
    but joy comes with the morning.

What I love about this psalm is the honesty that joy is a gift, and this gift is often in the context of great despair and sadness. The poet of Psalm 30 recognizes from the very beginning that we are in need of being "drawn up." It could be the poet needs to be lifted because others have subjugated him through abuse of power or privilege. Maybe his own sin or faults have him stooping low with a burden he can no longer carry. Perhaps he has taken the posture of a servant and has forgotten that being a servant means that he is the greatest of all. We don't know, nor do I think it matters. What matters is recognizing that it is God who does the lifting.

"Weeping may linger for the night, but joy comes with the morning." Weeping throughout the night feels like holding your breath, in a way. Time seems to stop, your pulse quickens, and your thoughts are singularly consumed. I find it interesting that Scripture is relatively silent on the details of Christ's birth. Luke records, "While they were there, the time came for Mary to have her baby. She gave birth to her firstborn child, a son, wrapped him snugly,, and laid him in a manger, because there was no place for them in the guestroom" (Luke 2:6-7). Compared with the context of Jesus' crucifixion, Luke's Gospel is relatively silent about Jesus' birth. Jesus isn't even named until he is presented in the temple eight days later. What a beautiful picture of the Trinity it would be to hear the details of Jesus' first breath, reminding us of the breath of life offered to humanity at the beginning of our story in Genesis.

But Scripture is silent about Jesus' behavior at his birth. Could it be that Jesus' birth wasn't as peaceful as "Away in a Manger" might have us think? "No crying he makes" might be an honest reflection, but it certainly isn't about peace. Panic begins if a baby is born without a cry. I've seen the seemingly infinite seconds between birth and a child's first cry, especially when the only sound in the room is doctors scurrying, nurses flailing, and questions left unanswered. Is Scripture silent because all of creation held its breath until the Christ cried? When we're weeping through the night like the psalmist and time seems to stand still, the story of Christ's birth can become a reminder that God holds God's breath with us. Joy is the steadfast assurance that God is with us.

Another Psalm, 139, begins with the words, "O LORD, you have searched me and known me" (NRSV). This deep, searching knowledge of God is a source of joy. God knows us better than we know ourselves, and the good news is that God still bothers to be our God. The psalmist goes on to say, "Even before a word is on my tongue, / O LORD, you know it completely" (NRSV). Some would ask, "Then what's the point?" One of my kids' favorite books begins, "In an old house in Paris that was covered with vines lived twelve little girls in two straight lines." Most of us know the story of *Madeleine*. That doesn't mean we only read it once. God knows the words that are on your tongue and in your heart, and you are called to share them. God is not a manager who is interested in the daily report. God is fundamentally interested in *you*. Saying "I love you" to my wife is not a conveyance of information; rather it is an investment in relationship. God knows what is on our heart, and the good news is that God is near and will take the time to listen anyway.

"You know when I sit down and when I rise up" (Psalm 139:2 NRSV). How purposefully mundane is that? I would expect that God would take notice of when we saved the company or reinvented public education or solved world hunger, and certainly God smiles because of the big stuff. But God is also there when we first open our eyes in the morning and when we close them at night. When we can find God in those moments between breaths, we begin to grasp at the depths of God's heart. We can find joy is the assurance that God is with us even in otherwise unremarkable moments.

Psalm 139:7-12 (NRSV) reminds us of God's constant loving presence with us.

> Where can I go from your spirit?
>> Or where can I flee from your presence?
> If I ascend to heaven, you are there;
>> if I make my bed in Sheol, you are there.
> If I take the wings of the morning
>> and settle at the farthest limits of the sea,
> even there your hand shall lead me,
>> and your right hand shall hold me fast.
> If I say, "Surely the darkness shall cover me,
>> and the light around me become night,"
> even the darkness is not dark to you;
>> the night is as bright as the day,
>> for darkness is as light to you.

It is easy to miss the scandal of presence the poet suggests. After God offered the Law to Moses and the ancient Israelites he commanded that they build a tent or tabernacle so that God could travel with them. Later after the kingdom was established, Solomon built a temple in which God could live. When the temple was in Jerusalem, God dwelled in the Holy of Holies. You would bring your sacrifice to the temple. You would bring your offering to the temple. You would go to God, in essence. The poet, here, doesn't mention the temple. He envisions God being outside of the temple—literally everywhere.

We like walls. We like boundaries and borders. It helps us define who we are and who we are not. Borders do have a purpose and are important, but they can be taken too far. Do we believe that God can be in both Israel and Gaza? Do we believe that God is in both Russia and Ukraine? Do we have faith that God is traveling with immigrant children forced to find a better way? Or does our reliance on boundaries and borders obscure our understanding? Can we with the psalmist also proclaim the scandal of God's unbound presence? If I make my bed on this side of the wall or that side of the wall, on neither side can I run from God's presence, and that should give us pause when tension escalates to violence. God is omniscient, unbound by human intellect. God is also omnipresent, unbound by the walls we build, whether the walls surrounding nations or buildings or the walls into which we put one another or the walls we build around our own heart.

Joy is the steadfast assurance that God is with us. If I ascend to heaven, when I'm enjoying the best of times, God is there.

When I make my bed in the pit, when I have hit rock bottom, God is there. When my soul leaps for joy God is there. This is the heart of an altogether joy.

Indescribable Joy

Sometimes joy is indescribable. Maybe it goes beyond "the steadfast assurance that God is with us." Have you ever tried to describe the indescribable? Years ago my daughter Isabelle asked me, "Daddy, why is yellow such a silly color?" I wasn't sure how to respond. I'm not sure if I would call yellow "silly." In fact, I'm not sure how to describe the color "yellow" at all. There is a beautiful book of poetry edited by Christian Wiman simply titled *Joy: 100 Poems*. He appropriately says in the introduction:

> If you are trying to understand why a moment of joy can blast you right out of the life to which it makes you all the more lovingly and tenaciously attached, or why this lift into pure bliss might also entail a steep drop of concomitant loss, or how in the midst of great grief some fugitive and inexplicable joy might, like one tiny flower in a land of ash, bloom—well, in these cases the dictionary is useless.[5]

Sometimes it's easier to describe what something is not. This is often the strategy John Wesley used in many of his sermons. For example, how might you describe the character of a Methodist? What sets a Methodist apart from disciples from other walks of faith? (At first blush I might say that Methodists are those who never shy away from singing in four-part harmony, always bring food to a meeting, and drink coffee as if there was a soon-to-be-announced worldwide coffee bean shortage.)

In John Wesley's "The Character of a Methodist," he spends several paragraphs saying what a Methodist is not. A Methodist is not someone of singular opinion. A Methodist doesn't use any distinguishing words or phrases. A Methodist is also not a follower of Christ who boils religion down to a singular cause. This doesn't mean Methodists are void of opinions, culturally identifying words, or great advocates for personal or social causes. Wesley is trying to say that being a Methodist will never rest in opinion, words, or causes. So what is a Methodist? A Methodist is one "who has the love of God shed abroad in his [sic] heart....God is the joy of his heart, and the desire of his soul."[6] He goes on to say that a Methodist is one who has hope, prays without ceasing, is pure in heart, produces good fruit, never speaks evil against a neighbor, and does good to all. In short, a Methodist is, well, a Christian.

It seems that John Wesley's desire was for a Methodist to be indistinguishable from any follower of Christ. It's rather boring to say that a Methodist simply is a Christian, but I think that's the point. If a Methodist is known for particular worship times, language about grace, song selection, dress, or greeting, then our identity is found in something secondary to Christ. It would be quite a blessing to be unable to describe our faith outside of the seemingly generic Christian tenets of peace, hope, love, and joy. This would mean that our faith and our expression of our faith are one and the same, or as Lisel Mueller compares it to, "two seemingly parallel lines / suddenly coming together."[7]

Joy is the steadfast assurance that God is with us, which means that joy rightfully experienced reveals that the line between creator and creation is thin. Joy is the moment we forget ourselves in the sacrificial love of the fully human and fully divine Christ. A moment of joy becomes harder to describe than our own consciousness. Just as I cannot prove myself to be, I cannot adequately describe joy. Experiencing joy and experiencing God are one and the same.

Think about God's name for a moment. Moses approaches the burning bush and asks, "If I now come to the Israelites and say to them, 'The God of your ancestors has sent me to you,' they are going to ask me, 'What's this God's name?' What am I supposed to say to them?" (Exodus 3:13). The Lord simply replies with a curious, "I Am Who I Am" (3:14). In other words, God is what it means "to be." God is life itself. When we find ourselves in a moment of joy, that moment that defies the simple categories of happiness or despair, that instant when time stops and we recognize our connectedness to one another, our world, and our Lord, what we are experiencing is the very presence of God. In other words, "we have neither an image nor a definition of God. We have only His name. And the name is ineffable . . . God begins where words end."[8]

This is why we light the candle of joy at the end of the season of Advent. Joy is where words fail. After all of the other candles have been lit; after the liturgy has been read; after the Christmas concerts, pageants, and budget meetings have been complete, all that's left is God in the flesh, the tangible presence of our assurance that God is with us. All that's left to do is point to the manger. This is why Mary "treasured and pondered" all that had happened on that "Silent Night." There's nothing else that needs to be done. An almost joy is too loud, feeling the necessity to fill the room with something—anything. An altogether joy needs nothing else. Joy is the experience of Christmas, "I Am." It is the presence of God that bolsters our exuberance and holds our lamentations near. Joy is the steadfast assurance that God is with us. There's nothing else we need to know.

Final Thoughts

Advent is always an exciting time for me. I hope I never tire of celebrating the anticipation of peace, hope, love, joy, and all that comes with it. The music, liturgy, visuals, and general good cheer that fill the sanctuary continue to contribute to moments where the church leans into its calling more so than at any other time of our shared liturgical heartbeat. Our sacred music spills out through radio stations and offices, the symbols of our faith are carried into living rooms and public arenas, and sharing the story of Christ seems as natural as mentioning the weather.

Maybe this is the picture of joy that we've been searching for. Seeing God's story in the world reminds us how often we think of the four walls of our sanctuary as a living room into which we are called rather than a springboard from which we are sent. God is with us at 8:30 on a Sunday morning, and at 9:00 a.m. in the office on Monday. Advent and Christmas help us see this connection where we have previously been blind. The world is in desperate need of joy, even if for just a moment.

Questions for Reflection

1. In what ways do you attempt to create joy during the weeks before Christmas? during other times?

2. Why do you think altogether joy is something that can only be received?

3. How can you open yourself more fully to receiving God's joy?

Hymn Reflection

"Hark! the Herald Angels Sing"
(*The United Methodist Hymnal*, 240)

In November 2018, SongSelect listed "Hark! the Herald Angels Sing" as the fifth most popular Christmas song of fifty-two hundred Christmas-tagged songs in their database. This carol has an overwhelming theme of altogether joy as the text wraps us up in the angels' message: "Glory to the newborn King!"

The hymn was originally published in *Hymns and Sacred Poems* of 1739; the first collection to contain one of Charles's hymns. The current *United Methodist Hymnal* combines six of the original ten verses to create three double verses and adds a repeat of the first verse's first line for a refrain. Many textual changes were also made over succeeding publications, many of which were complete by 1756. Most notably, the first line changed from "Hark how all the welkin rings!" to the familiar title we know today.

At its heart, the hymn recounts the story of the angels' visit to the shepherds to tell of the birth of Jesus. It is a call to the world to realize the power and fulfillment found in the infant Jesus. The first verse is an artful restatement of the words of the angels. "Glory to the newborn King; peace on earth, and mercy mild, God and sinners reconciled! . . . Christ is born in Bethlehem!" These quotations are interspersed with connective phrases that proclaim how we are asked to join in the celebration today, such as "Joyful, all ye nations rise, join the triumph of the skies."

The second verse defines who Jesus the Christ is: adored by heaven, our everlasting Lord, born of a virgin, god and man—veiled in flesh as incarnate Deity, our Emmanuel. It is important to note the full affirmation of faith about Jesus contained in this verse. This proclamation of who Jesus is continues into the third verse: "Prince of Peace, Sun of Righteousness! Light and life; healer," and then switches tone to express how Jesus acts in the world: he laid down his glory; he was born that we might have eternal life, to raise us to heaven, and to give us second birth.

The altogether joy that this hymn expresses complements John Wesley's final thoughts on being an altogether Christian. As believers sing this testament of faith, we agree with the angels that Jesus is all of these things; we believe that his actions are all of these actions; and we join with the angels in their joyous proclamation: "Glory to the newborn King!" This is an altogether joy!

EPILOGUE

AN ALTOGETHER COMMITMENT: WESLEYAN COVENANT RENEWAL

Many of us have our favorite Christmas movies and television shows. Among my most cherished childhood traditions was watching *Rudolph the Red-Nosed Reindeer*. You may know the story. The famous reindeer went on a trip with two traveling companions: Hermey the elf who wanted to be a dentist, and the wild-eyed explorer Yukon Cornelius.

The part that always enchanted me was when they found themselves in a place called The Island of Misfit Toys. It was a land filled with poor, rejected toys that no one wanted because there was something wrong with them. There was a toy train with square wheels, a water pistol that squirted jelly, a doll with low self-esteem, an elephant covered with spots—all of them banished to exile, shunned to the fringe of humanity, never to be chosen or loved.

I suspect this scene was in the show to teach children about empathy and compassion, to teach us not to judge others for their shortcomings because, in fact, all of us have them. And boy, did it work. I didn't know this, but when the show first debuted in 1964, the original show ended with the toys left on that island, never being rescued.

That ending elicited hundreds of angry letters from children from across the country after the show premiered. Children were so upset that the toys were left there, forgotten. So, the following year, the producers changed the script. They added a scene, a correction that became a new part of the show in 1965 and has been there ever since.

Now at the end of the show, Rudolph and Santa descend onto the island. Santa scoops them up, puts them into his bag, and loads them onto his sleigh, giving them to boys and girls around the world who eagerly receive them and give them the one thing they have always wanted and never had: the gift of love and acceptance.

Throughout this Advent season, at every stop along the way, we have discovered just how misfit our human condition really is. As much as God created us to be people of peace, hope, love, and joy, we are an imperfect people. At best, we are only able to achieve an "almost" kind of Christmas.

If we're honest, all of us are just a bunch of misfit toys.

Oh, I know, we don't want to admit it. We spend a lot of time and effort trying to project to other people that our lives are a lot better than they actually are. But you and I well know deep down inside that we have our own hang-ups, habits, and heartaches. We live in relationships that are broken, a past that is full of shame and guilt, and a future that is fraught with worry. We have the constant replay of old tapes in our minds that would convince us that we are far removed from the kind of life we know we should live.

If only someone could come and rewrite the script for us, to add a scene, to do for us what we cannot do for ourselves: to scoop us up and show us what unconditional love and second chances might look like.

Good news: that's the meaning of Christmas.

In Jesus, God became a misfit, just like us: a human being, susceptible to the same vulnerabilities that we face every day. God drew near to us, so that our story can have a new ending, one with hope and possibility, and the promise of new life.

There is just one thing we need to do in response: agree to come on board.

All those misfit toys had to do was jump into Santa's sleigh for an adventure that would change their lives. And according to John Wesley, that should be our response when it comes to Jesus: agree to follow him and commit our lives to him.

Renewing Our Covenant with God

In 1780, many years after the first covenant renewal service in Spitalfields, England, Wesley wrote a booklet called *Directions for Renewing Our Covenant with God*. It became the standard set of instructions for Methodists to use in preparation for their annual Watch Night Service at the start of every year. These spiritual instructions were a bridge between the season of Christmas and New Year's Eve and, in a certain sense, were a way for people to offer God the best Christmas gift of all: the commitment of their hearts.

In the preface of that booklet, Wesley did a bit of screen-writing himself, spinning a metaphor that feels a lot like the revised ending to Rudolph. He used a memorable phrase that captured for him what it meant to renew one's commitment to Christ, a phrase that you might adopt as your theme for the upcoming year, "Adventure yourselves in Christ":

> Adventure yourselves with him; cast yourselves upon his Righteousness, as that which shall bring you to God: as a poor captive exile, that is cast upon a strange land, a land of robbers and murderers, where he is ready to perish, and having no hope, either of abiding there, or escaping home with life.[1]

Wesley said that our sins have placed us in exile, in separation from God, basically putting us in a land of misfit toys. But there is hope, as God comes to us in Christ, as a rescue boat pilot who has come to save us:

> And meeting for a while with a pilot, who offers to transport him safely home, Jesus embarks on an adventure with him and everything he has in his vessel: you should do likewise. Christ offers, if you will venture forth with him, and then he will bring you home, and he will bring you to God.[2]

It may be that the best gift you have to give this Christmas is one you choose to give to God. It is a fresh commitment to follow Jesus, and a renewal of the covenant that God has made with you in Christ.

Wesleyan Covenant Renewal

Over the years, Methodists have started the new year with the observance of a Covenant Renewal Service, or Watch Night Service, on or around New Year's Eve. A full service is offered later that you might use for that purpose.

But even if you do not formally observe such a service, you would do well to take some time to consider John Wesley's five steps of preparation for covenant renewal, all taken from his instruction booklet:[3]

1. Confide in God

First, set apart some time, more than once, to be spent in secret before the Lord.

- In seeking earnestly God's special assistance and gracious acceptance of you.
- In considering distinctly all the conditions of the covenant, as they have been placed before you.
- In searching your hearts whether you either have already or can now freely make such a closure with God in Christ, as you've been exhorted to do.
- In special, consider what your sins are and examine whether you can resolve to avoid them all (even

those that most cross your interests and corrupt inclinations) as the rule of your whole life.

- Be sure you are clear in these matters; see that you don't lie to God.

To *confide* in someone means to "put full trust in" that person. It involves a willingness to be truthful and vulnerable with even your most guarded secrets. Confiding in God means taking off the masks that you so skillfully and diligently wear in front of others, in the confidence of God's faithful love.

Confiding in God therefore includes acknowledging and confessing your sins. It involves the delicate and difficult work of admitting your weakness, and declaring your dependence on God to overcome them. Doing so might make us uncomfortable, but Wesley did not allow shortcuts around this task. Confiding in God is not easy, but it is a critical first step.

2. Compose Your Spirit

Second, compose your spirits into the most serious frame possible, suitable to a transaction of very high importance.

After you have confessed your sins in confidence with God, you might be tempted to swing the pendulum completely in the other direction, saying to yourself, "Well, at least I'm not as bad as *so-and-so*." The tendency, then, is to compare ourselves with others, in an effort to inflate our self-esteem and preserve our own sense of dignity.

But Wesley cautions against such an overcorrection. He called us to "compose our spirits," which means to remember

114

that we are not the center of the universe. As Paul said, we are not "to think of [ourselves] more highly than [we] ought to think" (Romans 12:3). We should instead consider ourselves with sober judgment, remembering that we are all sinners, and all equally children of God.

3. Claim the Covenant

Third, grab hold of God's covenant and rely upon God's promise of giving grace and strength, whereby you may be enabled to perform your promise. Trust not your own strength nor the strength of your own resolutions, but take hold of God's strength.

We need to remember that the act of renewing our covenant with God is not initiated by our work, but comes from God. Wesley's image of "grabbing hold" of the covenant might be likened to a trapeze artist, who launches from a platform holding a trapeze bar. Mid-flight, the trapeze artist must make a choice, to let go of the bar and spin around midair in order to grab hold of the next bar.

For a few precious fractions of a second, the artist is in the middle of the air holding neither bar, sustained only by the hope that the other artist has released the other bar toward him, with just the right force at just the right time, so that when the time comes, the second artist can grab hold of it and swing safely to the other side.

This is what renewing our covenant with God is like. It means letting go of our sinful ways, as painful as that might be, in the full confidence that God has done all that is necessary to provide us the pathway to a renewed life.

4. Choose Faithfulness

Fourth, resolve to be faithful. Having engaged your hearts, opened your mouths, and subscribed with your hands to the Lord, resolve in his strength never to go back.

To "resolve" comes from the Latin word *resolvere*, which means "to loosen" or "to disintegrate." Resolving to be faithful means to daily loosen everything that would pull us back toward a life of sin and unfaithfulness and "never to go back." Think about how a marriage covenant is more than just the wedding ceremony, but a lifelong commitment to strengthen and sustain that marriage over the long haul. Wesley believed that one's covenant with God required a daily choice to follow God's will and be obedient to God's commandments.

5. Connect to God in Prayer

Fifth and last, being thus prepared, at some convenient time set apart for the purpose, get to work. In the most solemn manner possible, as if the Lord were visibly present before your eyes, fall down on your knees, and spreading forth your hands towards heaven, open your hearts to the Lord.

Prayer is the lifeblood of a person's relationship with God. It involves "opening your heart" to God in a set-aside manner, to both listen to God's voice and to share your heart with God.

Prayer is not some magical incantation, in which we elicit from God what we desire if we simply say the right words. It is more than just simple conversation, for sometimes we can pray without words.

Prayer, at its core, is an intentional attentiveness to God's spirit, "as if the Lord were visibly present before your eyes," and a recognition that God is always with us, always speaking, always listening, and always ready to guide us along the way.

An Altogether Christmas

There is no sense hiding from God the fact that you aren't perfect. You can go ahead and admit to yourself and to God that you've made mistakes, and that you feel like the chips are stacked against you to break free from this misfit life.

But the good news of Christmas is that God is here. God has come to you in Jesus, to be with you and tell you that you have not been forgotten, and that you are not alone. And God is calling you to a whole new adventure, in which you can follow Christ's lead, embody his example, and learn to love God and others.

It does not matter how hopeless the world might seem to you. God is with you to gives you an altogether hope, to set your soul on fire to go out and make a difference.

It does not matter how conflicted or how broken you might feel. God is with you to give you an altogether peace, so that you can let your life shine with the glory of God.

It does not matter what kind of life you have lived in the past. God is with you to give you an altogether love, so that you can have a chance at a brand-new start.

And it does not matter how long your journey has been, or how lost you might feel. God is with you to give you an altogether joy, and to tell you: Merry Altogether Christmas.

And welcome home, misfit. Welcome home.

A SERVICE OF COVENANT RENEWAL

From *One Faithful Promise*
by Magrey R. deVega
Based on "Directions for Renewing Our Covenant with God"
by John Wesley (1780)

Gathering

Call to Worship

LEADER: This covenant I advise you to make, not only in heart, but in word; not only in word, but in writing; and that you would with all possible reverence spread the writing before the Lord, as if you would present it to him as your act and deed: and when you have done this, set your hand to it: keep it as a memorial of the solemn transactions that have passed between God and you, that you may have recourse to it in doubts and temptations.

Opening Prayer

PEOPLE: O Most Holy God, for the sake of your Son, Jesus Christ, we offer ourselves to you as prodigals at your doorstep. We have fallen short because of our sins, and are prone to the wickedness and evil in the world. But you have promised mercy to us in Christ, and you call us to turn to you with all of our hearts. Therefore, by the call of your gospel, we come now, without reluctance, to submit ourselves to your mercy.

Opening Hymn
"A Charge to Keep I Have"

1. We Confide in God

LEADER: Having a full, life-giving relationship with God means putting away our idols, and being against that which God is against. Therefore, renounce those things from the bottom of your hearts, and in full covenant, use all the means that you know to refuse sin and corruption in your lives.

PEOPLE: O God, though we once were of the world, we now resign our hearts to you, humbly bowing before your majesty, with firm resolution in our hearts.

Scripture Reading

One or more of the following passages of Scripture are read: Jeremiah 31:31-34; Luke 9:18-27; 1 Peter 1:13-25; Colossians 3:1-14.

2. We Compose Our Spirits

Prayer of Confession and Assurance of Pardon

LEADER: Let us pray.

PEOPLE: O God, we wholeheartedly desire your grace, so that we might follow your call with resolve, forsake the world, turn away from sin, and turn to you. We will guard against all temptations, in good times and bad, lest they draw us away from you. We acknowledge our own powerlessness against such forces, and rely on your righteousness and strength.

(Silent prayer of confession)

LEADER: God is boundless in mercy and great grace, and offers us again to be our God through Christ. Therefore we solemnly pledge ourselves to God, bowing before God's majesty.

PEOPLE: We take you as our Lord Jehovah, Father, Son, and Holy Spirit. We yield our whole selves, body and soul, for your service, promising and vowing to serve you in holiness and righteousness every day of our lives.

Passing of the Peace

(Signs of peace and reconciliation are exchanged.)

Hymn of Preparation
"Come Let Us Use the Grace Divine"

3. We Claim the Covenant

Sermon or Other Word of Witness

Prayer of Commitment

LEADER: Since God has given Jesus as the only way to God, solemnly accept Jesus as the only new and living way, by which sinners may come to God. I call you to join in covenant with God.

PEOPLE: (The following is prayed in silence.) O blessed Jesus, I come to you hungry, wretched, miserable, blind, and naked. I am tarnished by sin, and my uncleanliness makes me unable to be in a relationship with you. But your love for me is unparalleled, so with all my heart I accept you, and take you to be my Lord, for richer and for poorer, for all times and conditions, to love, honor, and obey before all others, until my death. I embrace you in every way, renouncing my sinfulness, my wisdom, and my will, offering myself fully to you and taking your will to govern my life. And since you told me that I will suffer if I try to do this alone, I enter into a covenant with you, come what may. Your grace will assist me when I run into trouble, and I know that nothing in life or death will separate me from you.

The Wesley Covenant Prayer

LEADER: Let us pray this covenant prayer in the Wesleyan tradition.

PEOPLE: I am no longer my own, but thine.
Put me to what thou wilt, rank me with whom thou wilt.
Put me to doing, put me to suffering.
Let me be employed for thee or laid aside for thee,
exalted for thee or brought low for thee.
Let me be full, let me be empty.
Let me have all things, let me have nothing.
I freely and heartily yield all things to thy pleasure and disposal.

And now, O glorious and blessed God, Father, Son, and Holy Spirit,
thou art mine, and I am thine. So be it.
And the covenant which I have made on earth,
let it be ratified in heaven. Amen.

Sacrament of Holy Communion

4. We Choose Faithfulness

Prayer of Commitment

O God, Because you have been pleased to give your holy law as the rule of my life and the way I should walk in your kingdom, I willingly submit myself to you, set my shoulder to your burden, and subscribe in all your laws as holy, just, and good. I solemnly take them, as the rule of my words, thoughts, and actions, promising that though my flesh might contradict and rebel, I will try to order and govern my whole life according to your direction, and will not allow myself to neglect any of my duties to you. Now, Almighty God, searcher of hearts, you know that I make this covenant with you today without deceit or reservation, asking you, that if you see any flaw or falsehood in me, that you would reveal it to me and help me to get right with you.

Closing Hymn
"Jesus, United by Thy Grace"

5. We Connect to God in Prayer

LEADER: And now, glory be to you, O God the Father.

PEOPLE: From this day forward I look upon you as my God and Father, knowing that you are always looking for ways to recover sinners like me.

LEADER: Glory be to you, O God the Son.

PEOPLE: You have loved me and washed me from my sins in your own blood, and you are my Savior and Redeemer.

LEADER: Glory be to you, O God the Holy Spirit. By the power of your hand, you have turned my heart away from sin and back to you.

ALL: O holy and powerful God, Father, Son, and Holy Spirit, you are now my Covenant-Friend, and through your infinite grace, I am your Covenant-Servant. Amen. So be it. And the covenant which I have made on earth, let it be ratified in heaven.

Benediction

Depart in Peace

NOTES

Introduction

1   John Wesley, "The Sermons of John Wesley: Sermon 2 The Almost Christian," Wesley Center Online, accessed July 11, 2019, http://wesley.nnu.edu/john-wesley/the-sermons-of-john-wesley-1872-edition/sermon-2-the-almost-christian/.

2   John Wesley, "The Almost Christian."

Chapter 1: An Altogether Peace

1   Martin Luther King Jr., "When Peace Becomes Obnoxious," sermon delivered March 18, 1956, accessed July 12, 2019, https://kinginstitute.stanford.edu/king-papers/documents/when-peace-becomes-obnoxious.

2   Isaac Chotiner, quoting Martha Nussbaum, in "The Upside of Anger," *Slate*, August 6, 2018, accessed July 12, 2019, https://slate.com/news-and-politics/2018/08/anger-in-politics-when-does-it-work-and-when-does-it-backfire.html.

3   John Wesley, "The Sermons of John Wesley: Sermon 23 Upon Our Lord's Sermon on the Mount: Discourse Three," Wesley Center Online, accessed July 11, 2019, http://wesley.nnu.edu/john-wesley/the-sermons-of-john-wesley-1872-edition/sermon-23-upon-our-lords-sermon-on-the-mount-discourse-three/.

4   John Wesley, "Upon Our Lord's Sermon on the Mount: Discourse Three."

5   Gregory V. Palmer, sermon delivered to the Florida Annual Conference of The United Methodist Church, Lakeland, Florida, June 2018.

6   Christopher Klein, "World War I's Christmas Truce," History.com, October 15, 2018, https://www.history.com/news/world-war-is-christmas-truce-100-years-ago.

Chapter 2: An Altogether Hope

1   John Wesley, "The Sermons of John Wesley: Sermon 18 The Marks of the New Birth," Wesley Center Online, accessed July 9, 2019, http://wesley.nnu.edu/john-wesley/the-sermons-of-john-wesley-1872-edition/sermon-18-the-marks-of-the-new-birth/.

2   Dorothy Day, *Loaves and Fishes* (Maryknoll, NY: Orbis Books, 1963), 176.

3   John Wesley, letter to his brother Samuel, quoted in *The Life of the Rev. John Wesley, M.A.*, by John Whitehead (London: Stephen Couchman, 1853), 250, accessed July 13, 2019, https://books.google .com/books?id=ETZEAQAAMAAJ&printsec=frontcover#v= onepage&q&f=false

Chapter 3: An Altogether Love

1   John Wesley, "The Sermons of John Wesley: Sermon 139 On Love," Wesley Center Online, accessed July 11, 2019, http://wesley.nnu.edu /john-wesley/the-sermons-of-john-wesley-1872-edition/sermon-139 -on-love/.
2   John Wesley, "The Almost Christian."
3   John Wesley, "The Almost Christian."
4   Frank A. Thomas, "How to Preach a Dangerous Sermon," Schooler Institute on Preaching, February 12, 2019, Methodist Theological School in Ohio, https://www.mtso.edu/theologicalcommons /archive-resources/schooler-institute-on-preaching-2019/.
5   Frank A. Thomas, "How to Preach a Dangerous Sermon."
6   John Wesley, "The Almost Christian."

Chapter 4: An Altogether Joy

1   Christian Wiman, ed., *Joy: 100 Poems* (New Haven: Yale University Press, 2017), xxxvii.
2   John Wesley, *Free Grace: A Sermon Preached at Bristol*, 31-33, Internet Archive, accessed July 11, 2019, https://archive.org/details /freegracesermonp00wesl/page/31.
3   Christian Wiman, *Joy*, xiv.
4   Christian Wiman, xx.
5   Christian Wiman, xii.
6   John Wesley, "The Character of a Methodist," accessed July 11, 2019, Evans Early American Imprint Collection/Text Creation Partnership, https://quod.lib.umich.edu/e/evans/N20188.0001.001/1:3?rgn =div1;view=fulltext.
7   Lisel Mueller, "Joy," *Alive Together: New and Selected Poems* (Baton Rouge, LA: Louisiana State University Press, 1986), 199.
8   Abraham Joshua Heschel, *Man Is Not Alone: A Philosophy of Religion* (New York: Farrar, Straus & Young, 1951), 97-98.

Epilogue: An Altogether Commitment:
Wesleyan Covenant Renewal

1   Magrey R. deVega, *One Faithful Promise: Participant Guide: The Wesleyan Covenant for Renewal* (Nashville: Abingdon Press, 2016), various pages.
2   Magrey R. deVega, *One Faithful Promise.*
3   Magrey R. deVega, *One Faithful Promise.*

ALMOST CHRISTMAS

A Wesleyan Advent Experience

ALMOST CHRISTMAS
978-1-5018-9057-4

ALMOST CHRISTMAS: DVD
978-1-5018-9062-8

ALMOST CHRISTMAS: LEADER GUIDE
978-1-5018-9060-4

ALMOST CHRISTMAS: YOUTH STUDY BOOK
978-1-5018-9067-3

ALMOST CHRISTMAS: DEVOTIONS
978-1-5018-9069-7

ALSO FROM MAGREY R. DEVEGA
Awaiting the Already
Embracing the Uncertain

ALSO FROM MATT RAWLE
The Redemption of Scrooge
The Gift of the Nutcracker
What Makes a Hero?
The Grace of Les Misérables